Beowulf—
A Poem

PAST IMPERFECT

See further
www.arc-humanities.org/our-series/pi

Beowulf—
A Poem

Andrew Scheil

ARCHUMANITIES PRESS

British Library Cataloguing in Publication Data
A catalogue record for this book is available from the British Library

ISBN (print) 9781641893916
e-ISBN (PDF) 9781641893923
e-ISBN (EPUB) 9781641893930

www.arc-humanities.org
Printed and bound in the UK (by CPI Group [UK] Ltd), USA (by Bookmasters),
and elsewhere using print-on-demand technology.

Contents

Contents

Acknowledgements

Although this book was conceived, planned out in detail, and contracted prior to Covid-19, most of it was completed during the pandemic: initial work in spring of 2020, fully drafted over the summer, revised in January of 2021. So, I would like to thank Katherine Scheil and our two sons, William and David, as we tried to keep each other healthy and sane during what was a pretty strict quarantine for our household.

I would like to thank collectively the many students I have taught over the years for helping me slowly fashion and refine my ideas about *Beowulf*. Being cut off from face-to face teaching during the pandemic felt like being cut off from oxygen, and in some ways writing this book was a substitute for talking with students in a more normal fashion. Special mention goes to graduate students Jennifer Easler, Maggie Heeschen, Caleb Molstad, Karen Soto, Jesse Stratton, and Andrea Waldrep.

I would also like to thank a number of my own teachers and colleagues in Old English and medieval studies. Some heard about this book in progress; many did not. All helped me, directly and indirectly, either through their writing or personal friendship, or both: Bob Berkhoffer, Eddie Christie, Dan Donoghue, Janet Ericksen, Roberta Frank, Steve Harris, Mary Kate Hurley, Anatoly Liberman, Hal Momma, Jack Niles, Val Pakis, Andrew Rabin, Jana Schulman, David Townsend, Renée Trilling, Samantha Zacher. Bob Bjork helped me place this project with Arc Humanities Press; he has been a generous mentor and friend to all in the field for his entire career. Simon Forde has been the best of editors, and my gratitude to Rebecca Straple and the rest of the Arc Humanities Press editorial and production team as well. I thank the reader for Arc Humanities Press for their insightful, helpful comments. Parts of Chapter 2 (here re-written) were originally published as "*Beowulf* and the Emergent Occasion" in *Literary Imagination* 11, no. 1 (2008): 83–98.

I dedicate this book with love and affection to a very important person in my life: my aunt, Mary Ann Satter. A beloved high school English teacher (Brighton High School; Rochester, NY) with a long career (now retired), Mary Ann is and always has been a kindred soul as a devoted reader, feeding me books from my earliest age. In writing this, I was thinking of her voice in conversation and our shared love of reading.

Introduction

Now, perhaps more than ever, I read to find solace and meaning. And so, in the search for some shelter from "the wrackful siege of battering days," I submit *Beowulf*. My purpose here is simple: I want you to love *Beowulf*. I want you to find it as moving and significant as I do. For those who have not read the poem, this small book will serve as an invitation and introduction. For those who have read the poem, but found little of interest, this is a plea to reconsider. For those who already know and love the poem, I hope this short study will further deepen that pleasure.

Why should you bother to read *Beowulf*? This is not a flippant question. Life is brief and there are far too many good books to read in a lifetime, not to mention other pressing pleasures and responsibilities. What can reading *Beowulf* possibly offer? My answer: you should read *Beowulf* because it is a deeply humanist work; that is, *Beowulf* is a work of art that searches out, and attempts to address, the most fundamental question: what does it means to be human—medieval or modern—in this world around us? If reading is to be more than simple diversion, then for what other reason *should* we read, if not to be inspired and transformed and to test our sense of life's capacities? *Beowulf* needs to be championed as a moving literary experience; we need to understand (or be reminded) why Seamus Heaney called the poem a "work of the greatest imaginative vitality," a "work of art [that] lives in its own continuous present, equal to our knowledge of reality in the present time," a poem with an honoured "place in world art."[1]

Beowulf has been one of my companions for a long time. I'm quite sure my first introduction to it was sometime in the mid-1970s, when I was about ten years old, in the short but potent adaptation for children by Anne Terry White in *The Golden Treasury of Myths and Legends* (enhanced by the wonderful illustrations of Alice and Martin Provensen).[2] I first read and studied the full poem (in Michael Swanton's translation) in school when I was sixteen. Since then, I have read it for personal pleasure and taught it to a wide variety of students, in translation and in the original language, for over thirty years. I cannot, in fact, ever remember *not* having read or known *Beowulf* or having it as a part of my deeper self; Emerson's comment on his connection to Montaigne's *Essays* describes something of my own feelings about the poem: "It seemed to me as if I had myself written the book in some former life, so sincerely it spoke to my thought and experience."[3]

However, I certainly understand that mine is perhaps not the typical experience. Like so many great works, *Beowulf*'s appeal can be difficult, but we should not be hasty to dismiss difficult experiences, especially of books. We can be too quick to press the "like/dislike" button. In a well-known passage, Lionel Trilling turns this kind of judgement upside-down:

---

1 Seamus Heaney, "Translator's Introduction," in *Beowulf: A Verse Translation*, ed. Daniel Donoghue, 2nd ed. Norton Critical Edition (New York: Norton, 2019), xxiii–xxxix at xxiii and xxv. Hereafter abbreviated as "NCE."

2 *The Golden Treasury of Myths and Legends*, adapted by Anne Terry White, illustrations by Alice and Martin Provensen (New York: Golden, 1959).

3 "Montaigne; or, the Skeptic," in *The Annotated Emerson*, ed. David Mikics (Cambridge, MA: Harvard University Press, 2012), 326–47 at 334.

... a real book reads us. I have been read by Eliot's poems and by *Ulysses* and by *Remembrance of Things Past* and by *The Castle* for a good many years now, since early youth. Some of these books at first rejected me; I bored them. But as I grew older and they knew me better, they came to have more sympathy with me and to understand my hidden meanings. Their nature is such that our relationship has been very intimate.[4]

How refreshing I always find that passage! When we engage with a book, the experience is not one-way—not just the reader evaluating and judging the book. Rather, we interface with that entity we call "*Beowulf*," or "*King Lear*," or "*Pride and Prejudice*," and those books read us, as much as we read them. I do not feel I've ever been rejected by *Beowulf*, but it has taken decades of effort to more fully unlock the poem, to make myself the kind of reader worthy of the book. I hope these chapters will hasten that process for readers willing to make themselves open and vulnerable to that experience.

Therefore, I think of this book as a personal and appreciative literary introduction to *Beowulf*. This is not an introduction to the culture and history of early medieval England or to the broader literary culture of the period. I will stick very closely just to *Beowulf* in these pages and not head off into other works, which are likely to be unknown to the reader. This is also not an introduction to the scholarly study of *Beowulf*: there will not be typical discussion of the manuscript context, dating the poem, style and language, historical contexts, Christianity and paganism. There are many such scholarly introductions, whether in print or online; so no need to repeat them here.[5] Also, while such subjects have

---

4 Lionel Trilling, "On the Modern Element in Modern Literature," *Partisan Review* (1961): 9–35 at 15. The Trilling quotation is paraphrased and cited by Mark Edmondson in his wonderful book, *Why Read?* (New York: Bloomsbury, 2004), 46, essential reading for anyone who loves and teaches literature.

5 Three key works that can propel anyone into the deeper scholarly study of the poem are the following: R. D. Fulk, Robert E.

inherent interest, they say little or nothing about the poem as an abiding literary experience. It is easy to cloud this crucial matter with background information and scholarly debates, and yet never confront the more pressing issue right in the foreground: why bother to read it? I believe the reading of literature should be a transformative endeavour, and I believe *Beowulf* is as subtle, affecting, and moving as any great work of world literature.

"Beowulf, Monster-Slayer"

Many readers at this point might say "well, I already know *Beowulf* and I like/don't like it." But chances are, no matter your impression (positive or negative), what you are calling *"Beowulf"*–the entity you carry in your head—bears only an oblique relationship to the actual Old English poem. Far more people know "the story of Beowulf" without having read the poem. And that is wonderful! The vibrant academic field of reception history has taught us that some works can break free of their inceptive historical contexts of time and place to then circulate as "world literature": in translation, adaptation, revision, parody.[6] These endless adaptations are not "debasements" of a more worthy pristine "original." As Chris Jones shows in a fine essay on *Beowulf* adaptations, even the one manuscript copy of the poem we have is itself a derivation from a prior version, and from a prior version before that, and then back into the distant prior world of pre-literate art. There is no one "original" and "authentic" *Beowulf* and then a host of false adaptations;

Bjork, and John D. Niles, eds. *Klaeber's Beowulf*, 4th ed. (Toronto: University of Toronto Press, 2008); Robert E. Bjork and John D. Niles, eds. *A* Beowulf *Handbook* (Lincoln: University of Nebraska Press, 1997); Andy Orchard, *A Critical Companion to* Beowulf (Cambridge: Brewer, 2003).

6 This definition of "world literature" is from David Damrosch, *What is World Literature?* (Princeton: Princeton University Press, 2003). On adaptations, see Linda Hutcheon, *A Theory of Adaptation*, 2nd ed. (New York: Routledge, 2013).

we have rather an endless circulation of infinite variety, each of these iterations potentially worthy of study and enjoyment.[7]

But one effect of this process is that the circulated "public image" of *Beowulf* is invariably a partial rendering of the extant medieval work. While powerfully generative of new adaptations, this cultural meme we call *"Beowulf"* is inevitably a reduction of the medieval poem. Almost without exception, every adapted form of *Beowulf* concentrates mostly on the monster-fights only. Therefore, *Beowulf* becomes "Beowulf, Monster-Slayer" and little else. Even when the medieval text is taught in the classroom, it is generally the case that the limited time spent on the poem is directed mostly to the monster fights and a rather simplistic view of heroism; much of the poem's complexity does not conform easily to classroom instructional time.

The public image has therefore generally eclipsed the medieval text: "Beowulf, Monster-Slayer" is much better known (and consequently hated or beloved) than *Beowulf*, the Old English narrative poem from the early Middle Ages. What is lost in that simplification? What I would call the humanist dimension of the poem. We lose, for example, the all-important narrator, whose presence considerably deepens the complex humane effect of the work. We also lose all the allusive, dark, complex material of the "digressions." Stripped of all this, when someone says they know *Beowulf*, this tends to be the *"Beowulf"* they know—"Beowulf, Monster-Slayer." The monsters are important, and J. R. R. Tolkien definitively changed the course of our understanding of the poem in his celebrated 1936 essay on the monsters.[8] But in my view, the

---

7 Chris Jones, "From Heorot to Hollywood: *Beowulf* in its Third Millennium," in *Anglo-Saxon Culture and the Modern Imagination*, ed. David Clark and Nicholas Perkins (Cambridge: Brewer, 2010), 13–29. One can include in this sense the recent creative feminist reimagining of the poem by Maria Dahvana Headley in *The Mere Wife* (New York: Farrar, Straus, and Giroux, 2020) and in *Beowulf: A New Translation* (New York: Farrar, Straus, and Giroux, 2020).

8 J. R. R. Tolkien, *"Beowulf*: The Monsters and the Critics," (1936);

monsters are only a gateway to the more rewarding and complex human concerns of this stately work.

My goal therefore is to introduce you to a great and strange work of verbal art from a vanished world. Let's try to suspend thoughts of "Beowulf, Monster-Slayer" and try to read the poem without preconceptions. If it helps, in order to de-familiarize the poem and see it anew, pretend, as long as you can, that its title is anything but *"Beowulf"*; scholars only gave it that title in the nineteenth century anyway. Call it *Song of the Ancient North* or *Deeds of Light and Darkness* or anything else that might stir your imagination.

Scholars, Critics, and the Love of Beowulf

So the phenomenon of "Beowulf, Monster-Slayer" in the popular consciousness probably helps explain why the reading of the poem (in translation) can be a disappointing experience for most—if you are expecting "Beowulf, Monster-Slayer," then when you get to the actual poem, there are a lot more lines devoted to speeches and confusing exposition than there are to monsters and action. But what have the professional scholars, critics, and teachers been doing with this poem? They are the ones who are supposed to mediate it to the broader public. The record, unfortunately, is mixed. The critical history of *Beowulf* is quite odd. Unlike Chaucer and Shakespeare, for example, whose works had their literary champions during their own lives and immediately after their death, and then found that reputation enhanced by several hundred years of scholarship and criticism and popular readership, *Beowulf* was unknown to posterity for a very long time. *Beowulf* had no real critical reception until the nineteenth century. This is not the place for a full critical history of *Beowulf* scholarship, but the first thing to note is that there was (and continues to be) a long tradition of scholars who read and study and value the

repr. in NCE, 111–38. On the monsters see Andy Orchard, *Pride and Prodigies: Studies in the Monsters of the* Beowulf-*Manuscript*, 2nd ed. (Toronto: University of Toronto Press, 2003).

poem, but mainly for non-literary reasons: *Beowulf* is very important to historians; to linguistic specialists; to scholars of manuscripts and oral-formulaic poetry; to archaeologists, and more.[9] And this too, is a wonderful thing! The achievements of scholars in these disciplines and their work on *Beowulf* over the past few hundred years is inspiring: may it ever continue. But it has meant that quite a bit of work on the poem in these demanding disciplines does not, understandably, attend much to the poem as a literary experience for a more casual reader.

Even to begin to understand the technical subjects of *Beowulf* scholarship requires long, noble specialist training. For all these scholars, their primary reason to study the poem is often to illuminate other, non-literary, concerns. Questions of literary worth become secondary or invisible. And then, by extension, quite often "to teach" *Beowulf* is to teach descriptively *about it* and to teach *about its contexts* and its scholarly issues; not so much to re-create its literary effect in an act of critical empathy and understanding. We should be able to treat *Beowulf* like any other great work of literary art that reads *us* as we read it, without retreating into contextual information to avoid such an encounter. It is understandable to want to have power over a text, to explain its ambiguities, and solve its puzzles. We want to impose our will on a work, rather than letting it work its will upon us, opening up to it, letting its vitality operate inside us. But such an open perspective requires humility and vulnerability. We should allow a text to challenge and change us. And so, occasionally, we must step back from *Beowulf*'s endlessly compelling scholarly puzzles, and ask "What is this work's vision of human experience? What questions does it pose, how does it present them, and how does it answer them, if at all?" And then to ask: "Given the poem's total complex vison of humanity and the world, can you, reader, use it? What happens when you measure your own

---

9 See T. A. Shippey and Andreas Haarder, eds. *Beowulf: The Critical Heritage* (London: Routledge, 1998).

view of the world and your own inner self against the poem's experience?"[10]

There have been scores of talented *Beowulf* scholars who have illuminated its many enigmas. But, by my reckoning, there has been a much thinner line of academic critics who have read the poem with the sensitivity and nuance that I long for (at least in print—the classroom may be a different matter). The first among them is Tolkien. As is well known in the field, Tolkien's polemic essay established *Beowulf* as a complex work of literature; as Bruce Mitchell (perhaps over-optimistically) noted long ago, since Tolkien's lecture, the work "is now viewed more as a poem and rather less as a museum for the antiquarian, a sourcebook for the historian, or a gymnasium for the philologist."[11] Tolkien's essay is justly celebrated, but it is also true that it probably has had an oversized influence on the poem's understanding. My debt to the essay (and the critical tradition it initiated) is apparent throughout this book, but I try to walk around this influence, so to speak, conscious that one is always in its shadow. At all times, I write with the conviction, so energetically advocated recently by Rita Felski, that literary criticism at the present moment needs to bring out all the positive encounters with literature: inspiration, invention, solace, recognition and identification, reparation, passion, consolation, empathy and sympathy, creation and enchantment, the "eros of love and connection."[12]

To sum up: lots of views out there on "Beowulf, Monster-Slayer"; many superbly talented specialist scholars of the poem; relatively few excellent literary critics of *Beowulf*. So I write this little book to exalt a work of art that I feel has very few effective literary advocates at the moment; there

---

10 Cf. Edmondson, *Why Read?*, 56.

11 "'Until the Dragon Comes ...': Some Thoughts on *Beowulf*" (1963); repr. in Bruce Mitchell, *On Old English* (Oxford: Blackwell, 1988), 3–15 at 3.

12 *The Limits of Critique* (Chicago: University of Chicago Press, 2015), 17, *passim*.

is a lot of accomplished technical scholarship in print, also some quite bad attempts at criticism, but not much to make you love the poem, or explain why you might find the reading experience moving and worthwhile. My goal is to gather up the best that I think has been thought and said about the poem as a literary experience, and supplement that with my own thoughts. In the end, I write this not only for the reader who wants to appreciate *Beowulf*, but I write this also especially for the unnamed *Beowulf*-poet, who laboured hard and long over these words, who cared enough to bring a complex creative vision into being. I want to conjure up a loving vision of what the experience of the poem is like, a critical re-creation that the poet would perhaps find satisfying.

The Humanist *Beowulf*

What do I mean when I call *Beowulf* a "humanist" work of art? What do I mean by "humanism" in this regard? I am obviously not using the term in a historically specific way: this is not a book about a Renaissance or Enlightenment reception of *Beowulf*. Rather, I find a congruence between the values and perspectives of modern humanism (which of course has its historical roots and transhistorical character) and the literary endeavours and effects of our poem.[13] To unpack this assertion in greater detail is the task of the following pages, but here are the main emphases; *Beowulf* is a humanist work because:

- it is interested in and engaged by the lives of real human beings in the here-and-now of this terrestrial world (i.e., it is not a visionary work like Dante's travels to the afterlife, or the exotic travelled-to spaces of romance);

- it is interested in and engaged by human ways of knowing, human understanding, human beliefs and customs;

---

13 For introductions to humanism in this sense see Tony Davies, *Humanism*, 2nd ed. (London: Routledge, 2008) and Stephen Law, *Humanism: A Very Short Introduction* (Oxford: Oxford University Press, 2011).

- it is interested in and engaged by the conduct of human life, human ethics and morality, at both the individual and collective (or social) levels;

- it is interested in and engaged by the varied ways individual human lives are embedded in and conditioned by social institutions and history;

- it is interested in and engaged by existential and meta-physical concerns (e.g., the afterlife), to the extent that these relate to lived human experience;

- as the poem, in its length, mediates upon the above subjects, it displays at all times a complex (sometimes conflicted), searching curiosity and intelligence.

In this list, I mean "interested in and engaged by" to stand for a variety of ways the poem treats these subjects. Questions, doubts, meditations, assertions, contradictions, gnomic proc-lamations, hortatory injunctions, argumentation: the poem uses all these and more to explore the enigmas of the human story. *Beowulf* does not, in its totality, present one clear, uni-vocal argument about anything (humanist or otherwise). At all times, it presents a vivid exploration of the human experi-ence: from birth to death, lingering on each moment for itself, each moment of human engagement fully regarded, deeply felt and apprehended.

In order to make my case that anyone can and should read *Beowulf*, I use Seamus Heaney's acclaimed poetic translation for all citations, and only occasionally discuss a few lines or words in Old English.[14] At the moment, Heaney's translation is probably the most widely known and read English translation

---

14 All references will be by lines numbers of the translation in the Heaney *Beowulf* Norton Critical Edition ("NCE"); the Heaney translation has been reprinted in a wide variety of formats: as the NCE; as a stand-alone volume; with facing-page Old English; in a wonderfully illustrated volume (ed. Niles); in the many editions of the *Norton Anthology of English Literature*. If I cite any Old English, it is from Klaeber.

of *Beowulf*. The translation is also a work of modern poetic art in its own right by an important modern poet, and if one of the purposes of this book is to get more people to read and appreciate *Beowulf*, then I believe the Heaney translation conveys a compelling but accessible, aesthetic power.[15]

In other words, another argument here is that the poem does not necessarily need to be read in the original language to find it deeply provoking and satisfying. *Beowulf*'s humanist art transcends the translation process. Of course, the poem is certainly *even more* startling and powerful in the original language, and each time I teach it to students in Old English, I am reminded of this and my appreciation grows deeper every year. But an argument for the excellence of the poem in Old English would proceed in a very different way. The sad fact is that only a vanishingly tiny percentage of people will ever read the poem in Old English; I want to make my case to the larger audience who might read it in translation.

Each of the following four chapters makes the case for a humanist *Beowulf*. Although the chapters do build on each other in sequence, I have fashioned them also to be stand-alone studies, the better to be read or used in various ways. Annotation is kept to a very bare minimum, in keeping with the Past Imperfect series. Chapter 1 is about doubt, an essential ingredient in any humanist enterprise. Chapter 2 is about the poem's interest in the contingency of human events. The poem's atmosphere of doubt and its complicated perception of contingency leads to the tragic mode, the subject of Chapter 3. Chapter 4 argues that a powerful counterpoint to the tragic mode of the poem is its delight in art, making, and the cunning of form: the eloquent poem, the beautiful ship, the intricately wrought sword and cup. Set against the darkness of the poem is the bright delight in human skill and its infinite faculties.

---

15 For an analysis of Heaney's translation as poetry, the best places to start are his illuminating "Translator's Introduction" in NCE, xxiii–xxxix and Daniel Donoghue's "The Philologer Poet: Seamus Heaney and the Translation of *Beowulf*," in NCE, 230–41.

Beowulf is, in many ways, unique. While it is thoroughly traditional and of its age, it is also *sui generis* and a highly original, even experimental work of verbal art.[16] The poem's survival from the past, and its current world-wide ubiquity—the capacity now to find a translation easily, and read it, and to fall into the poet's imagined world—is nothing less than miraculous.

Beowulf: A Summary

I provide here, as a preliminary to our literary conversation, a compact summary of some basic scholarly facts and questions about *Beowulf*. *Beowulf* is the modern title given to a long anonymous and untitled narrative poem of 3182 lines written in the earliest form of the English language ("Old English"). The poem exists in only one manuscript copy made around the year 1000, somewhere in England. This surviving copy derives from an antecedent copy (and probably more than one), in a transmission process going back some number of centuries. The poem was composed in England, but exactly who wrote it; when, where, and how it originated; how many copies or versions stood between any "original" and our surviving early eleventh-century copy are all subjects of scholarly debate.

The entire poem (the work of one poet) is a legendary/semi-historical fiction set not in medieval England, but in various more ancient locations in Scandinavia and northern Europe. It is clear that the poem uses ancient techniques of poetry, storytelling, and subject matter; it is part of what

---

16 I am not alone in this assessment; e.g., commenting on the narrative structure of the poem, Michael Lapidge notes that in terms of *Beowulf*'s narrative devices "there is no satisfactory model in antecedent western literature"; and "[o]ne could even say that no medieval poem—in Latin or in the vernacular—composed before *c.* 1100 bears any resemblance to *Beowulf* either in its structure or in its narrative discourse" ("*Beowulf* and Perception" (2001) in NCE, 242–68 at 256, 260).

must have once been a large body of vernacular Germanic poetic storytelling across the North Sea region, now mostly vanished, but with enough surviving in later medieval versions in various languages for us to understand much about this literature. The narrative of *Beowulf* is set in the period just prior to the Middle Ages: the pre-literate, pre-Christian north of the fifth and early sixth centuries. Characters and events in the poem range from the historical to semi-historical/legendary to fantastical.

The evolution of the poem seems to have begun with a core body of legendary material originating in Denmark connected to a great sixth-century hall complex at Lejre on Sjælland (the island on which Copenhagen stands). This body of legendary material appears to have had two main subjects: first, the travails of the Scylding (Old Norse *Skjöldungar*) line of Danish kings; and second, the haunting of their hall by a monster. The monster-haunting very soon was assimilated to a folktale motif: the so-called "two-troll" narrative, in which a hero defeats two successive monstrous attackers of a settlement.

This complex of legendary/folktale material then migrated to England. When? Either relatively early (late seventh or early eighth century), or somewhat later (after the mid-ninth century). Once in England, other details, sub-plots, and digressions accrued to the original body of material: e.g., the dragon fight, the name "Grendel," the characters' Scandinavian names were Anglicized, the Breca swimming contest, and so forth. When, or in what order these elements were added, and by how many stages, we do not know. Most of these details were probably added to the main story-complex when it circulated in oral transmission (perhaps in poetic form, perhaps not), but we cannot be sure.

And then, at some English time and place (seventh-century East Anglia or Northumbria?, eighth-century Mercia?, the ninth-century Danelaw?), someone conceived of a project to compose and set down in writing a long Old English poem capturing all this material, in traditional oral-poetic style and subject matter, using the figure of a central hero named "Beowulf" to write a sophisticated poem that foregrounded the stories of this hero's killing of the two troll-like monsters in his youth, and his death as a king in old age while slaying a dragon, with briefer reference to other exploits among his people, the Geats.

But the poet augmented this central story matter in at least two important ways: first, by embedding these monster-slaying moments in Beowulf's life within a complex body of other allusive tales and legends scattered throughout the main narrative—other stories: told, partially told, or simply referred to throughout the work; and, second, by providing a complex narrator to preside over the poem and comment regularly upon the action: a distinct voice with traits deriving both from the secular poetic tradition and from the early medieval Christian world-view. *Beowulf* is a complex and rich poetic enterprise generated in early Christian medieval England, but looks back to its pre-Christian past; it is a retrospective poetic fiction, not a barbaric pagan story simply "brushed up" and transmitted by pious Christian monks.

And this poet—deeply skilled in the composition of Old English poetry in a traditional style rooted ultimately in pre-literate oral art—somehow saw this grand-scale endeavour committed to parchment. Why and how was this done? Who (or what institution) precipitated this project? Was it a literate Christian poet, who was nevertheless also well-skilled in traditional secular verse? If so, how did this person come by these skills and how did he operate? (Most likely the poet was a "he," but is there any possibility it was a "she"?) Could the project have been a collaboration between a non-literate, skilled oral poet and others who were able to set it down into writing and burnish it? Or was it something else? Such questions, once again, are the subject of scholarly disagreement. Once composed and set down in writing, the work then began its long journey (how many centuries and intervening copies, we do not know) to the final extant latter-day copy from the early eleventh century. What happened along the way? Was the poem altered, augmented, or rewritten? In small or large ways? All fascinating scholarly questions, but our subject here: is it worth reading?[17]

---

[17] My summary of this probable evolution of *Beowulf* from its origins in Denmark to our single manuscript copy of the poem, follows in general the arguments of John D. Niles in "On the Danish Origins of the *Beowulf* Story," in *Anglo-Saxon England and the Continent*, ed. Hans Sauer and Joanna Story, with Gaby Waxenberger (Tempe: Arizona Center for Medieval and Renaissance Studies, 2011), 41–62, summary of the evolution at 56–61; see also see the related materials and essays assembled by Niles in *Beowulf and Lejre* (Tempe: Arizona Center for Medieval and Renaissance Studies, 2007).

Chapter 1

Doubt

A central premise for any humanist perspective is that doubt is the all-important ingredient for understanding the world and our place in it; that the acceptance of doubt—uncertainty, dubiety, ambiguity—is the beginning of knowledge and wisdom.[1] Doubt enables thinking and reasoning; unquestioned certainty is, by contrast, a precondition for stasis and ignorance. Another version of this humanist precept is the Socratic cliché that ignorance is the beginning of wisdom; that understanding the limits of human knowledge is the precondition for a considered life.

I would also argue that a kind of doubt plays an important role in our engagement with literature. As Milan Kundera noted, literature allows us to try on "experimental selves"; at the moment of reading, a new perspective opens up for the reader as they interface with the literary text and sample its experience. This elusive moment may be consciously or unconsciously perceived; it may be slight or great; but the encounter is unavoidable in reading. In that illumination, the reader briefly measures the experience they find in the text (whatever that may be) against their own deepest self—registering doubt (if only for a moment), as they try on that different, experimental self. Now, that moment of doubt may be

---

1 See Jennifer Hecht, *Doubt: A History* (New York: Harper Collins, 2003) for a broad popularizing overview of doubt in religion and philosophy.

imperceptible or have no real effect. But it may also be something grander and transformative. The history of reading is
filled with many such moments ("this book changed my life"),
but the glory is that this kind of transformation is an everyday
marvel. If any kind of literary encounter produces doubt of
this kind, how much more so, when doubt itself is an explicit
element of the literary experience, as in the case with *Beowulf*.

Now, if you've read *Beowulf*, you might not think doubt
plays much of a role. Do not the voices of *Beowulf* tend to
speak in absolute terms, and not in doubtful ones? "It is
always better / to avenge dear ones than to indulge in mourning" (1385–86): Beowulf's resolute expression of the heroic
code. Or a similar absolute metaphysical declaration voiced
by the narrator: "The truth is clear: / Almighty God rules over
mankind / and always has" (700–702). These do not seem
to be expressions of doubt. Yet when we look more closely
into the poem and measure its many voices, one against the
other, we find, in that complex, evolving totality not univo-
cal declarations only, but a chorus of conflicting voices and a
doubtful search for meaning.

This chapter will show several ways doubt traverses
Beowulf. We will examine the poem's tendency to offer differ-
ing narratives of the same events; isolate several regularly
deployed rhetorical features that promote doubt; see how
the poem foregrounds the limits of human knowledge; and
then show how this all culminates in the doubts surrounding
Beowulf's death.

Doubt: Alternate Narratives

Beowulf generates doubt through the poem's disconcerting
tendency to offer competing narrative versions of events.
As Fred Robinson summarizes: "[r]epeatedly we are asked
to listen to one account of an event and to compare it with
another."[2] For example, early in the poem, after Beowulf's

---

2 Fred Robinson, *Beowulf and the Appositive Style* (Knoxville: University of Tennessee Press, 1985), 25.

introduction at Heorot, Hrothgar's spokesman Unferth challenges Beowulf's monster-slaying credentials:

> "Are you the Beowulf who took on Breca
> in a swimming match on the open sea,
> risking the water just to prove that you could win?
> It was sheer vanity made you venture out
> on the main deep. And no matter who tried,
> friend or foe, to deflect the pair of you,
> neither would back down: the sea-test obsessed you.
> ... he outswam you,
> came ashore the stronger contender." (506–12, 517–18)

Unferth concludes: "So Breca made good / his boast upon you and was proved right" (523–24); his verbal challenge is a traditional feature of ancient Germanic literature: a *flyting*, that is, a traditional verbal "combat" used to sound out a character's heroic credentials.[3] Unferth accuses Beowulf of being nothing less than a failure and a fraud, not up to the task at hand.

Following the conventions of this verbal contest, Beowulf then answers the challenge by telling a different version of the Breca story, at greater length and detail, and with an opposite conclusion:

> Beowulf, Ecgtheow's son, replied:
> "Well, friend Unferth, you have had your say
> about Breca and me. But it was mostly beer
> that was doing the talking. The truth is this:
> when the going was heavy in those high waves,
> I was the strongest swimmer of all." (529–34)

In Beowulf's expansive re-telling of the story we get far more information than in Unferth's version. Beowulf tells us that the two young warriors grew up together; that they were

---

3 Carol Clover, "The Germanic Context of the Unferth Episode" *Speculum* 55 (1980): 444–68. For a broader context see Ward Parks, *Verbal Dueling in Heroic Narrative: The Homeric and Old English Traditions* (Princeton: Princeton University Press, 1990).

armed with swords against sea-monsters; and that they were
evenly matched until storms drove them apart:

> But Breca could never
> move out farther or faster from me
> than I could manage to move from him.
> Shoulder to shoulder, we struggled on
> for five nights, until the long flow
> and pitch of the waves, the perishing cold,
> night falling and winds from the north
> drove us apart. (541–48)

Beowulf's version of the tale then expands even further, telling us that sea-monsters attacked him:

> The deep boiled up
> and its wallowing sent the sea-brutes wild.
> My armour helped me to hold out;
> my hard-ringed chain-mail, hand-forged and linked,
> a fine, close-fitting filigree of gold,
> kept me safe when some ocean creature
> pulled me to the bottom. Pinioned fast
> and swathed in its grip, I was granted one
> final chance: my sword plunged
> and the ordeal was over. Through my own hands,
> the fury of battle had finished off the sea-beast.
> Time and again, foul things attacked me,
> lurking and stalking, but I lashed out,
> gave as good as I got with my sword. (548–61)

Beowulf then finally brings his version of the narrative to an
end:

> Light came from the east,
> bright guarantee of God, and the waves
> went quiet; I could see headlands
> and buffeted cliffs. Often, for undaunted courage,
> fate spares the man it has not already marked.
> However it occurred, my sword had killed
> nine sea-monsters. Such night-dangers
> and hard ordeals I have never heard of
> nor of a man more desolate in surging waves.
> But worn out as I was, I survived,

came through with my life. The ocean lifted
and laid me ashore, I landed safe
on the coast of Finland. (569–81)

Thus, two antithetical versions of the contest with Breca, side
by side: which one is true? Of course, the narrative weight of
the text favours us privileging Beowulf's account: he is clearly
the heroic protagonist and the hero's version must be correct,
yes? But in the flow of the narrative moment, if one sits in
the place of the reader, one version of this tale (Unferth's) is
delivered and understood; and then another competing version (Beowulf's) is delivered and understood. Unferth raises
doubts about Beowulf's capacities, doubts about the honorable reputation of the stranger boasting before the Danes;
honour in the world of the poem is a construct that itself is
fragile and subject to continual revision. Unferth tells a story
that casts doubt on that reputation. Beowulf answers those
doubts with his own more powerful story. But, for a moment,
the simple narrative placement of one event (the swimming
contest) with two competing parallel representations of that
event, must generate doubt for the reader. Which account,
we want to know, was true? The desire for certainty is not just
a modern reader's preoccupation: Beowulf himself explicitly
says he will correct Unferth and declare the true (*soð*) story.

A second example of doubt and alternate narratives
occurs when Beowulf returns to his homeland after his successful adventures at Heorot. When Beowulf and his men settle in at Hygelac's court, the king asks him, in the presence of
all, what happened on his adventure:

"How did you fare on your foreign voyage,
dear Beowulf, when you abruptly decided
to sail away across the salt water
and fight at Heorot? Did you help Hrothgar
much in the end? Could you ease the prince
of his well-known troubles? Your undertaking
cast my spirits down, I dreaded the outcome
of your expedition and pleaded with you
long and hard to leave the killer be,
let the South-Danes settle their own

blood-feud with Grendel. So God be thanked
I am granted this sight of you, safe and sound."
(1987–98)

Questions and doubts characterize Hygelac's speech here.
We, the audience, know what has happened, but Hygelac and
the Geat court does not yet. However, even before Beowulf
answers Hygelac's questions, for the attentive reader or listener this speech does not quite add up. Earlier in the poem
we had *not* been told that Hygelac "pleaded" for Beowulf to
stay home or that Hygelac "dreaded the outcome." Instead,
earlier the narrator had stated the exact *opposite* sentiment
regarding Beowulf's journey:

[Beowulf] announced his plan:
to sail the swan's road and search out that king
[Hrothgar],
the famous prince who needed defenders.
Nobody tried to keep him from going,
no elder denied him, dear as he was to them.
Instead, they inspected omens and spurred
his ambition to go ... (199–205)

Well, which is it? Was Beowulf encouraged to go, or was he
dissuaded? Such inconsistencies can be found in any long pre-
modern work, and particularly in works with some relation to
oral tradition and folktales.[4] Is the poem's contradiction here
intentional or accidental? In the end, from the reader's perspective, it does not really matter, since the *effect* is the same:
the inconsistency creates a momentary space of reasonable
doubt when two very different narratives are produced for
one set of events. We have our doubts, if only for a moment.

But this initial flash of doubt increases as Beowulf then
proceeds to re-tell his own exploits to Hygelac and the court:
a one-hundred and sixty-three-line re-telling of his Danish
adventure (1999–2162). Once again, as with the Unferth episode, as readers we process two competing narratives of the

---

4 On the folktale patterns underlying *Beowulf* see T. A. Shippey, "The
Fairy Tale Structure of *Beowulf*," *Notes and Queries* 16 (1969): 2–11.

same events: one version we have already experienced, told by our presiding narrator in the main action of the poem; and now a second version, told from the more limited perspective of one character and participant. Beowulf begins by telling of the hopeful mingling of Geats and Danes in Heorot before the night of Grendel's attack, matching closely with what we have already been told. But then his narrative diverges unexpectedly and Beowulf gives us something new and important—that Hrothgar's daughter Freawaru was there with Queen Wealhtheow distributing mead in the hall, a "young bride-to-be / to the gracious Ingeld, in her gold-trimmed attire" (2024–25). The marriage of the young woman to Ingeld, legendary king of the Heathobards, was intended to heal hostilities between the two peoples, but Beowulf is skeptical of this plan. To illustrate his doubts about the marriage's potential for peace-weaving, Beowulf then postulates, in a vivid digression, about what he thinks will *probably* happen in the future: at Ingeld's court the Danes accompanying Freawaru will mingle with the Heathobards; at some point, someone (an old warrior who remembers the history of the feud), will spot a sword on the hip of a Dane, a Heathobard sword plucked as a trophy on the field of battle; this old warrior will whisper in the ear of that dead man's son, urging him to vengeance. Eventually and inevitably, the peace brought about by a new bride will break down. None of this important information, this grim political prophecy, was presented to us during the earlier narrative version of the feast. It is new information that, given how dark and dire it is, necessarily leads one to doubt retroactively the authority and primacy of the first version.

The abrupt introduction of a major character and her story—Hrothgar's own daughter—is a bit of a jolt. Why wasn't she mentioned the first time this scene was narrated? Again, in the world of pre-modern literatures such concerns are perhaps irrelevant—we are dealing with folktale-style narrative sequencing, perhaps, rather than anything like a modern realistic novel. But certainly one effect, regardless of cause, is that at the introduction of Freawaru's tale, the mind inevitably travels back to that earlier version of the story, remembers the divergence, and registers a momentary doubt.

Beowulf resumes the re-telling of his own story, with a variety of new details. We learn the name of the first Geat killed by Grendel in his attack (Hondscio, 2076). Beowulf tells us that as Grendel reached for him, the troll carried a sack made of dragon-hide to carry off his prey, a detail absent from the first version (2085–88). Beowulf relates the celebrations at Heorot after his victory and the entertainment by the Danish *scop*; but we also learn that Hrothgar himself (among others) took turns improvising tales at the harp:

> There was singing and excitement: an old reciter,
> a carrier of stories, recalled the early days.
> At times some hero made the timbered harp
> tremble with sweetness, or related true
> and tragic happenings; at times the king
> gave the proper turn to some fantastic tale,
> or a battle-scarred veteran, bowed with age,
> would begin to remember the martial deeds
> of his youth and prime and be overcome
> as the past welled up in his wintry heart. (2105–14)

Freawaru, Hondscio, Grendel's dragon-skin sack, Hrothgar's own skill as a performing poet: none of these vivid and arresting details illuminated the first narrative version of these events. Again, regardless of what the incipient cause is for these divergent narratives, the effect is clear: some dissonance, contradiction and, therefore, doubt as the reader attempts to navigate these variations. Just what is the relationship of these competing representations to the events they purport to describe? Where is the truth in this world of competing narratives?

Doubt: "as I have heard tell ..." and "no one knows ..."

Both of these large-scale narrative alternates—the stories of the swimming contest with Breca and Beowulf's report to Hygelac—call attention to these tellings as *re-tellings*: iterative verbal acts of re-creation and transmission that by their very nature are potentially imprecise, partial, doubtful. The re-telling of known stories relates to two rhetorical devices that I would like to turn to now. Doubt in the poem is generated not only at the large scale of competing narratives, but also at the small scale of verbal details. Two of these rhetorical patterns emphasize the limits of human knowledge, and therefore doubt: the poem's "[I] heard tell" formulas, and its "no one knows" formulas. These expressions are a part of the poet's overall interest in the process of human cognition and understanding; Lapidge summarizes: "one of the poet's principal concerns was epistemological: the processes of acquisition and evaluation of knowledge, of the mental perception of an event rather than the event itself, and the arrangement of these mental perceptions in a narrative structure."[5]

It might sound as if I am claiming *Beowulf* is something like a postmodern novel, with similar experimental challenges to truth-telling; but the fluid and iterative nature of medieval storytelling is completely conventional: that is, the process whereby stories are not owned exclusively by any one author (in the era long before copyright), but are re-made through the channels of tradition, with each new, enriching telling. Because such stories are fluid and multiple by nature, their truth-claims are re-tested with each new telling. Even the first words of the poem signal this mode of storytelling: the first three lines declare the subject of the poem to be the glory of the Danes and their kings long ago: "We *have heard* of those princes' heroic campaigns" (3). We all know the stories of the legendary glory of the Danes; sit down to hear another version. And as re-told stories, stories revivified, they owe no particular allegiance to one set of stable truths. Such a putative, absolute consistency would be more likely the jurisdiction of books, with their set facts, records, and evidentiary claims. Unlike many other Old English poems, *Beowulf* never even once mentions books or writing in any way as sources of information or narrative, only the "hear-

---

5 Lapidge, "*Beowulf* and Perception," 261.

ings" of oral tradition.[6] These refences to oral/aural information transmission have been fully assimilated to the literate world of Anglo-Saxon poetry in *Beowulf*; however, the poem still bears the stamp of this oral tradition in many ways. All such tales have the potential for doubt, because multiplicity and potential inconsistency are part of their nature.

Consider the following cluster of words and expressions that constitute the "heard tell" formulas: two closely related verbs, *fricgan* and *gefrignan*, both meaning "learn" or "learn by inquiry and hearing"; the derived adjective *gefræge*, "well-known, because heard tell of after oral inquiry"; and the noun *gefræge*, "information learned aurally through oral inquiry." This last noun is part of a well-known poetic formula *mine gefræge*, which might be translated very literally as "according to my information that was learned by ear, through oral inquiry." The usual translation for *mine gefræge* is "as I heard tell"; this phrase and other related expressions are translated by Heaney in a variety of ways throughout the poem. They underwrite the action throughout, producing an atmosphere of (potential) hearsay. The narrator tells us that Beowulf "heard about Grendel ... over in Geatland" (194–95). When Beowulf and his men arrive in Denmark, the coast guard who asks who they are; Beowulf in turn asks him if what they have heard is true—that something haunts the king's hall (273–77). When Beowulf himself speaks to Hrothgar in Heorot, he says the same thing: "news of Grendel, / hard to ignore, reached me at home: / sailors brought stories of the plight you suffer" (409–11). That which is "heard tell of" may, by its very nature, possibly not be true, and is subject to doubt. It is true that

---

6 For the oral tradition and its relationship to *Beowulf* and to literacy, begin with John D. Niles, Beowulf: *The Poem and Its Tradition* (Cambridge, MA: Harvard University Press, 1983) and his *Homo Narrans: The Poetics and Anthropology of Oral Literature* (Philadelphia: University of Pennsylvania Press, 2010); Mark C. Amodio, *Writing the Oral Tradition: Oral Poetics and Literate Culture in Medieval England* (Notre Dame: University of Notre Dame Press, 2004), 1–78.

"as I heard tell" could be understood as an endorsement of certainty, rather than doubt—that is, the weight and force of prior oral tradition as a validating authority. But I believe that both responses are possible—doubt and certainty—within the ambit of the formula's meaning. And at any rate, "as I heard tell" is fundamentally different and more ambiguous than "as books tell us," the more usual appeal to stable authority in Old English texts.

In *Beowulf*, knowledge is obtained by word of mouth; the poem itself is aware that this system of knowledge is an imperfect thing and leaves room for doubt and limits to human knowledge. This brings us to our second rhetorical device: another common expression in the poem is "no one/ man knows." We see this expression in the prologue of the poem, the life and death of Scyld Scefing. The narrator tells us that God sent Scyld to the Danes alone, as a "foundling" (7) who would be their saviour, and that when his death came they loaded him on his funeral ship "and he crossed over into the Lord's keeping" (27). But who exactly sent Scyld to the Danes and who received his body at the end of his life are left ambiguous. The poet tells us that upon his death Scyld's people

> ... decked his body no less bountifully
> with offerings than those first ones did
> who cast him away when he was a child
> and launched him alone out over the waves. (43–46)

Who are these "first ones" (Heaney's translation of *þe hine æt frumsceafte forð onsendon*, "[those] who sent him forth at the beginning [or "at his birth"])? Their ambiguity is matched by the ones who received Scyld's death ship; the Danes send their king back into the unknown,

> ... let him drift
> to wind and tide, bewailing him
> and mourning their loss. No man can tell,
> no wise man in hall or weathered veteran
> knows for certain who salvaged that load. (48–52)

"No man can tell ... who salvaged that load": who (or what), exactly, sent Scyld to the Danes at his birth? Who (or what) took him back at his death? Similarly, when Grendel is introduced and his domain described, the narrator reflects that "nobody knows" where these monsters dwell (162–63). We find doubt generated at the macrolevel of the narrative, with competing versions of important events; we also find doubt attending the microlevel of the poem's diction, with its epistemological formulas: "I heard tell ... but no man knows ...."

Doubt: Narrator Knowledge and Character Knowledge

We should apply here a third doubt-inducing aspect of *Beowulf*, this one based on the poem's distinctive use of its narrator or narrative voice. The characters within the poem have a far more limited sphere of knowledge than does the narrator (and by extension, the audience).[7] The narrator knows things that characters do not, and makes sure the reader is aware of this discrepancy. For example, the narrator explicitly tells us that the Danes did not realize their desperate offerings at pagan shrines to ward off Grendel were a useless "heathenish hope" (179). He tells us that Beowulf's men do not know that Grendel has magic invulnerability to normal weapons (793–804). He tells us that the Geats had no idea a dragon lay concealed, curled around the treasure of a long-dead race (2270–86). This dichotomy between the narrator's expansive knowledge and the characters' more limited perception creates much of the poem's complexity and sophistication. Not many medieval texts are built this way and there

---

7 What I here call "the narrator," Stanley Greenfield called, in a classic essay, "the authenticating voice" of the poem ("The Authenticating Voice in *Beowulf*" (1976) repr. in *Hero and Exile: The Art of Old English Poetry*, ed. George H. Brown (London: Hambledon, 1989), 43–54; Greenfield sees one of the main functions of the "authenticating voice" as to present an emphasis on the limits of human knowledge (52).

are many consequent effects, beyond what I attend to here; but certainly one important consequence of this dichotomy is to highlight the problem of knowledge, and therefore, once again, of doubt.

Let's look in detail at a vivid and well-known example of this structure: the narrator's knowledge of Grendel's origin vs. the characters' understanding. The characters in the poem do not know that Grendel and his mother are the cursed descendants of the evil brother-slaying Cain, part of a long line of monstrous progeny at war with God since the beginning of time. The narrator, however, has a detailed authoritative knowledge of their origin, telling us that

> [Grendel] had dwelt for a time
> in misery among the banished monsters,
> Cain's clan, whom the Creator had outlawed
> and condemned as outcasts. For the killing of Abel
> the Eternal Lord had exacted a price:
> Cain got no good from committing that murder
> because the Almighty made him anathema
> and out of the curse of his exile there sprang
> ogres and elves and evil phantoms
> and the giants too who strove with God
> time and again until He gave them their reward. (104–14)

And the narrator's similar comments on Grendel's mother:

> Grendel's mother,
> monstrous hell-bride, brooded on her wrongs.
> She had been forced down into fearful waters,
> the cold depths, after Cain had killed
> his father's son, felled his own
> brother with a sword. Branded an outlaw,
> marked by having murdered, he moved into the wilds,
> shunned company and joy. And from Cain there sprang
> misbegotten spirits, among them Grendel,
> the banished and accursed ... (1258–67)

Now compare this detailed explication of the monsters' origin with the characters' lack of knowledge. For all the characters, the monstrous attacks are cloaked in obscurity and doubt. Early in the poem, the Danes grow desperate from the attacks in the night—always at night, in the shadows of ignorance:

> All were endangered; young and old
> were hunted down by that dark death-shadow
> who lurked and swooped in the long nights
> on the misty moors; nobody knows
> where these reavers from hell roam on their errands.
>
> (159–63)

The "dark death-shadow" accurately renders *deorc deaþ-scua*; the phrase, like much of the language used to describe Grendel and his mother is indistinct and metaphorical. The words and circumlocutions used to designate the monsters and their attacks reflects the uncertainty of the characters as they again and again try to understand what is happening to them in the dark night: "There was panic after dark, people endured / raids in the night, riven by the terror" (192–93). Beowulf's explanation to the coastguard of what he knows or has heard about the creature is vague and searching:

> "So tell us if what we have heard is true
> about this threat, whatever it is,
> this danger abroad in the dark nights,
> this corpse-maker mongering death ..." (273–76)

Finally, after the attack of Grendel's mother, Hrothgar tells all assembled (and the reader) what they know of the creatures, and it is a vague and meagre dossier:

> "I have heard it said by my people in hall,
> counsellors who live in the upland country,
> that they have seen two such creatures
> prowling the moors, huge marauders
> from some other world. One of these things,
> as far as anyone ever can discern,
> looks like a woman; the other, warped
> in the shape of a man, moves beyond the pale
> bigger than any man, an unnatural birth
> called Grendel by country people

> in former days. They are fatherless creatures,
> and their whole ancestry is hidden in a past
> of demons and ghosts." (1345–57)

Clearly an intentional contrast is being drawn here between Hrothgar's assertion that the ancestry of the creature is hidden and unknown and fatherless, and the narrator's clear and specific knowledge of the ultimate father of the Grendel-kin—Cain, the primal kin-slayer and murderer. Through these and many other moments the narrator displays a deeper knowledge than the characters; in the total experience of the poem, the reader vicariously experiences both perspectives, knowing and unknowing. This dichotomy cannot help but foreground doubt. The poem very clearly arranges things so that we regularly see characters *not knowing*, and *not understanding*, struggling in the dark, both literally and figuratively.

The narrator's greater knowledge does not simply displace the doubt or uncertainty of the characters' more limited perspective. Even if the narrator can lay claim to greater authority as far as truth, in these moments the simple duality of these two perspectives signals the presence of doubt for the reader. This effect (really a kind of irony) is part of the poem's humanist perspective: the placement of these two perspectives in "conflict" forces the reader to negotiate them, thus foregrounding the search for knowledge as an essential human activity.

Doubt: Beowulf's Death

Let us end by examining the doubtful uncertainties surrounding Beowulf's death. When the dragon appears unexpectedly and burns Beowulf's own hall to the ground, the poet gives us an extraordinary pause, taking us inside Beowulf's mind for a moment:

> Then Beowulf was given bad news,
> a hard truth: his own home,
> the best of buildings, had been burnt to a cinder,
> the throne-room of the Geats. It threw the hero
> into deep anguish and darkened his mood:

> the wise man thought he must have thwarted
> ancient ordinance of the eternal Lord,
> broken His commandment. His mind was in turmoil,
> unaccustomed anxiety and gloom
> confused his brain … (2324–33)

What is the exact nature of this "unaccustomed anxiety and gloom"? The Old English says, more literally, that his "breast welled inside with dark thoughts" (*breost innan weoll / þeostrum geþoncum*). The general sentiment is clear, but what is this "ancient ordinance of the eternal Lord," and how might Beowulf have broken it, if he indeed did so? The poem is ambiguous on this point. However, for our purposes what is important is that whatever the transgression is that Beowulf thinks he *might* have committed, he is *not sure* if he has done so. He is in doubt. A lesser poet adapting this heroic material would not have our hero pause, Hamlet-like at this moment. He would just have Beowulf get on with it. But our poet gives our hero (and us) this poignant and enigmatic moment of mental doubt, "as was not customary for him" (*swa him geþywe ne wæs*).

There are more doubts accompanying Beowulf's death as it plays out in slow motion. When the messenger goes to report Beowulf's death to his people, the narrator tells us that they have been waiting, in doubt whether their king would live or die:

> that crowd of retainers
> who had sat all morning, sad at heart,
> shield-bearers wondering about
> the man they loved: would this day be his last
> or would he return? (2893–97)

Their doubt seems to exemplify the narrator's important reflective passage a little further on, which muses that no one knows how, when, or where life will end:

> Famous for his deeds
> a warrior may be, but it remains a mystery
> where his life will end, when he may no longer
> dwell in the mead-hall among his own.

> So it was with Beowulf, when he faced the cruelty
> and cunning of the mound-guard. He himself was
> ignorant
> of how his departure from the world would happen.
> (3062–68)

The passage expresses a central truth of the poem: that doubt characterizes human life. It is a "mystery," a *wundur* (the word can also mean marvel, wonder, miracle), where and when the allotted life (*lifgesceafta*) of a man famous for his deeds (*eorl ellenrof*) will reach an end; when he can no longer live (*buan*) in the mead-hall (*meduseld*).

And finally, there are doubts about what happens, exactly, to Beowulf after his death. The narrator is a bit vague about this:

> For the son of Ecgtheow, it was no easy thing
> to have to give ground like that and go
> unwillingly to inhabit another home
> in a place beyond; so every man must yield
> the leasehold of his days. (2587–91)

"To occupy a home elsewhere" (*wic eardian / elles hwergen*) is a metaphoric, but evasive, way to represent where Beowulf goes after death. At the moment of death, the narrator tells us where Beowulf's soul goes: "His soul fled from his breast / to its destined place among the steadfast ones" (2819–20); in Old English: *him of hræðre gewat / sawol secean soðfæstra dom*. What this sentence exactly means is a famous ambiguity in the poem. The Old English phrase *soðfæstra dom* has at least three problems. First, *dom* can mean a variety of things: "judgement," "determination," "decree," "authority"—especially in Christian contexts, as in "the judgement (*dom*) of God"; however, the word can also mean something more secular: "glory, fame, or honour"—texts speak of the glory or fame (*dom*) of a good sword or a warrior. Second, there is also a simple problem with the syntax: *soðfæstra* is a genitive plural, giving us "the judgement of those firm in truth." But how does this "of" work? Is this a subjective genitive ("judgment by those firm in truth" upon Beowulf) or an objective genitive ("judgment upon those firm in truth" i.e., such as Beowulf)? Is he going to be judged *by* those steadfast in truth or is he *one* of those steadfast in truth? Third, who exactly are "the ones firm in truth"? The dead heroes of old in some indeterminate afterlife? The saints and angels and company of the just in heaven? It is difficult to say whether the ambiguity is deliberate or not. What we can say is that the poet could have said something much more straightforward: "his soul went to heaven" or "his soul sought the bosom of Christ" or "his soul found the keeping of Jesus."

Beowulf's death is characterized by a deliberate understatement and restraint that continues in the subsequent death scenes. Beowulf's own final words, to Wiglaf alone, are exquisitely sparse and ambiguous.

> "You are the last of us, the only one left
> of the Waegmundings. Fate swept us away,
> sent my whole brave highborn clan
> to their final doom. Now I must follow them."
>
> (2813–16)

This final sentence is even more stark and simple in Old English: *ic him æfter sceal.* "I must (go) after them," with the verb of motion unexpressed, but understood. It is pithy understatement comparable to Hamlet's final words to Horatio: "The rest is silence."

But where does this passage say Beowulf goes after death? He must follow all the other extinct Wægmundings, wherever they went: fate (*wyrd*) swept (*forsweop*) his kin away *to metodsceafte*, which Heaney translates as "to their final doom." This is a legitimate translation, but it is another ambiguous phrase: Klaeber glosses this as "decree of fate, death"; it is also possible that it means "at their appointed destiny, i.e., time appointed for death." Again, whatever the solution to this scholarly puzzle (if it is not deliberate ambiguity), what is clear again is that Beowulf could have been clearer or simpler, and said something like "All the Wægmundings are gone, taken by death" or even "All our kin are dead; now I join them." The poetic expression here is ambiguous and contributes to the pattern of doubt surrounding Beowulf's death.

I hope that I have shown that doubt is related to the poem's complexity of design. The poem is reflective, meditative; it encompasses, in the totality of its poetic expression, a great multitude of voices and perspectives. Doubt is both cause and effect: the poet intentionally built doubt into the fabric of his work; and doubt is an important part of the experience of the work, for reader or listener. Doubt establishes the proper humanist foundations for the explorations to come in the following chapters and doubt harmonizes with the poem's curious emphasis on the contingent nature of human affairs, subject of the next chapter.

Chapter 2

Contingency

Doubt therefore permeates *Beowulf* in a variety of ways and this spirit of questioning is part of the poem's existential concerns. But could anything seem more contrary to the popular image of *Beowulf*—that it is a meditative work of existentialism? But it is true: *Beowulf* is a reflective poem, concerned with the large questions of human existence: Who are we? What is this world that we find ourselves in? Are we alone? How does this world work and what is the part I am to play in it? Is there a divinity that shapes our ends, rough hew them how we will? Or does humanity prey upon itself, like monsters in the deep?

I would like to show in this chapter how *Beowulf* poses and explores these humanist questions through its interest in the contingent nature of human events. What do I mean by "contingent" in this sense? That the poem is centrally concerned with unexpected events; with the way events are connected to each other in unexpected ways; with the way events relate to one another in the movement of causality. And, finally, in the implications of contingent events: does a higher power direct the movement of human lives by some design, no matter how obscure; or is life simply driven by human choice in the world, and all its random joys and sorrows. Who makes the world?

Change and the Emergent Occasion

Change has always been the presiding author of our lives. Whether incremental or swift, unexpected or foreseen, change demarcates our perception of time and time's ongoing narrative expression. We live according to the narratives, the stories, that give our lives sense and form. Changing circumstances—especially sudden, unexpected changes—stress or rupture our expectations of normality and reality. We respond to the force of these emergent occasions in various ways in order to accommodate what Donne called the "[v]ariable, and therefore miserable condition of Man."[1] It is at those moments of pause and change that human individuality is perhaps felt most keenly; the reverberations of the emergent occasion play about the border between individual lives and their enveloping contexts. *Beowulf* is the earliest text in the English tradition that takes the emergent occasion and its effect on human lives as one of its central concerns. Through its representation of unprecedented change, *Beowulf* deliberates upon a pressing humanist issue: the formation of human character in the exigency of the contingent moment. Our poet sets his characters and his audience in a world of secure knowledge and expectations, and then he tracks the complex effects produced when unexpected change disrupts their lives.

My focus is on those narrative moments when an awareness of imminent change rises to a self-conscious point; when the inevitability of transition gathers itself and the rhetoric of a narrative pauses to survey past, present, and future in a single moment of pause. What is important here, in other words, is that moment of transformation, when it is made clear that a nexus of change beckons, or is at hand, or recedes now steadily into the distance of memory. I have in mind those fascinating spaces of suspension and slow time, when the world seems to stand still for a moment before plunging on, that interval, that significant season, to use Frank Kermode's

---

1 John Donne, *Devotions Upon Emergent Occasions*, ed. Anthony Raspa (Oxford: Oxford University Press, 1987), 7.

phrase.[2] Just as Macbeth periodically stops to ponder his frustrated desire to know the future in the present instant, so too the *Beowulf*-poet allows moments of reflection upon the contingency of events to enter his interwoven narratives. As he stands before the spectre of the emergent occasion, Macbeth gives voice to the dreadful inertia of causality: "I am in blood / Stepped in so far that, should I wade no more, / Returning were as tedious as go o'er" (III.iv.137–39). Our poet is drawn to similar moments of reflection when confronted by the contingent nature of events. We have already seen that the *Beowulf*-poet is a philosophical artist fascinated by epistemology and doubt; he is also a poet of contingency, a poet of the emergent occasion.

This chapter will first show the extent of the *Beowulf*-poet's preoccupation with unprecedented change: a fascination with the turn of events layers the narrative in rich and complex ways, beyond a simple use of the medieval mutability topos.[3] Further, this preoccupation has a studied effect upon the audience (reader or auditor, medieval or modern): it produces a series of rhetorical pauses as readers and characters within the narrative contemplate the ongoing mystery of contingency and causality in human affairs. In the end, I suggest that through this rhetoric of novelty the poet develops a more complex representation of human individuality in the poem than is generally seen in literature of the early Middle Ages, part of its humanist project. At moments of unprecedented change the poet attempts to give us literary characters seen not as static figures, but rather as complex human lives subject to historical contingency.

---

2 Frank Kermode, *The Sense of an Ending: Studies in the Theory of Fiction* (Oxford: Oxford University Press, 1966), 46.

3 Almost every thematic study of *Beowulf* seems to discuss mutability at some point; see, e.g., Phyllis R. Brown, "Cycles and Change in *Beowulf*," in *Manuscript, Narrative, Lexicon: Essays on Literary and Cultural Transmission in Honor of Whitney F. Bolton*, ed. Robert Boenig and Kathleen Davis (Lewisburg: Bucknell University Press, 2000), 171–92 at 183–86.

Unexpected Events and Outcomes

In the interwoven paths of its entire complex narrative, the
Beowulf-poet delights in the errant and surprising course of
events. Here we see the advantage of the poem's unusually
broad temporal scale: as the poet depicts several generations of interrelated lives, this allows him to contextualize
Beowulf's monster fights within a complex web of precedent
and outcome, a lattice of historical events as subtle and
meditative as the monster fights are bloody and garish. For
example, events or characters of little initial promise turn out
later to end up very important indeed. Scyld's arrival begins
the poem on a note of the unexpected, as does his success
as a glorious king: who would have thought that from such
humble beginnings—a foundling adrift on the sea, without
family ties—he would grow to such a fearsome king? Beowulf's success in Denmark is perhaps just as unexpected as
Scyld's. Hygelac tells us that his young retainer "abruptly"
(1988) decided to take up his adventure to Heorot; the Geat
king tried to dissuade him, thinking a positive outcome for
the journey unlikely (1992–97). Beowulf, after all, is the son of
Ecgtheow—a man who had been an exiled outlaw for his slaying of Heatholaf and was only saved by the intervening, generous hand of Hrothgar (371–76, 459–72). That Beowulf, son of
an outlawed exile and also a man seen as lazy and timid in his
youth (2183–88), surely such a man could not save the Danish
kingdom and later even become king of the Geats?

Just as the young Beowulf turns out in the end unexpectedly better than the promise of his youth and paternity
might imply, so too does Wiglaf, the young hero left alone
at the end of the poem, follow a similar path. The untried
Wiglaf helps Beowulf defeat the dragon; however, Wiglaf also
is an unexpected success. Buried in the complex "digressions" of the poem's second half we learn that Wiglaf's father
Weohstan was also a man with a dubious past, at least from
the Geat perspective: Weohstan fought on the side of the
Swedes in their war against the Geats. Weohstan stood with
the Swede Onela, the murderous slayer of his own brother,
King Ohthere; looking to finish the job of wiping out rivals to

the throne, Onela invaded the Geat kingdom searching for the heads of his brother's sons, Eanmund and Eadgils, who had been sheltered by Hygelac's son King Heardred. Onela kills Heardred (in other words, kills Beowulf's lord and king) and Weohstan kills Eanmund and claims his sword as a trophy. Later (in a way left unclear by the poem), Weohstan's son Wiglaf becomes a member of the Geats and is in fact the only retainer to stand by Beowulf against the dragon. Wiglaf ultimately kills the monster with Eanmund's sword, handed down as treasured battle-spoil from father to son, the all-important weapon used to pierce the dragon's hide when Beowulf's own sword failed. Therefore, who could have predicted that Wiglaf, an untried young warrior in his first rush of battle (2625–27), a man whose father was at one time an enemy of the Geats, would turn out to be the *one* loyal retainer to stand with Beowulf against the dragon and save the Geats from the fire? Apparently, our poet wishes to show that good (and evil) can come from unlikely or unpredictable sources across the generations, and that the contingent implications of events can only be seen (if at all) in a broad span of time.

Our poem also tracks the unforeseen reverberations of events that are certainly thought to be significant at their inception, but then twist and turn in the years to come in utterly unpredictable ways: the consequences of sheltering exiles, for example. Hrothgar befriends an exiled outlaw named Ecgtheow, pays his criminal debt (*wergild*) and befriends him for little apparent reason. Years later, that man's son, Beowulf, arrives to help the king in his moment of greatest need, past and present suddenly meeting. According to the world of medieval heroic narrative, offering shelter to an exile is not an insignificant act; and in Hrothgar's case that moment of generosity later made all the difference. But again, in the poem's complex and enigmatic second half we see that similar acts can have darker outcomes. Heardred, Hygelac's ill-fated son, offers sanctuary to the exiled Swedes Eanmund and Eadgils. As we saw above, that decision does not work out as happily—Hygelac was behind their grandfather Ongentheow's death, giving Onela more than enough reason to invade Geat territory in search of his nephews. Onela kills Heardred (payback for an earlier generation's attack), clearing the way for Beowulf to receive the throne. By sheltering exiles, in other words, Heardred brings about disaster and his own death, but in the larger context his self-destructive actions also clear the way for Beowulf's long, glorious reign, and through the consequent journey of Eanmund's sword from the dead Swedish prince to Wiglaf's hand, ultimately enable the slaying of the dragon. In its interwoven plot, our poem invites us to marvel that, as Tolkien put it in another context, "even the very wise cannot see all ends."

And so, as contingent occasions follow their strange, sometimes ironic course and ripple between past and future, our poem pushes the audience to look backward and forward at the same time, moving between analepsis ("flashback") and prolepsis ("flash-forward"). In this way the poem dramatizes the way understanding itself works, what the philosophers call "the hermeneutic circle": when the onset of novelty, the unexpected experience, races back down the corridor of our formerly held preconceptions, altering our subsequent base of preconceptions as the new event is assimilated to our understanding of the world and our ideas of what *could* happen. What our poem seems to be drawn to is the immeasurable moment before the hermeneutic circle completes its circuit. In the emergent occasion, time stands still for a moment: in the shock of its advent such a moment seems completely unforeseen and scrambles our understanding of what is possible and understandable. But then, in its wake, such an emergent event attains an air of inevitability as the workings of its causality become clear, assimilating to our hermeneutic framework and then informing our new preconceptions going forward.

Defeated Expectations

Therefore, as the poem delights in showing, expectations can be treacherous. *Beowulf* consistently undermines expected outcomes, as if responding to a certain tragedy of human

understanding. Precedents describe, if anything, only prob-
ability; preunderstanding is only half of the hermeneutic
circle, yet it is the only half we have access to before the
leading edge of experience. Something truly new is literally unimaginable—until it happens and then is imaginable.
Beowulf constantly dramatizes the unexpected betrayal of
precedent understanding, those startling moments when the
unexpected happens. For example, old and proven swords
such as Hrunting and Nægling fail for the first time, not biting
in their expected manner. This is not simply mentioned in
passing: the poet lingers over these failures. For example, in
a moment of pause he sets up the pedigree and abilities of
Hrunting, "a rare and ancient sword" (1458), in detail:

> The iron blade with its ill-boding patterns
> had been tempered in blood. It had never failed
> the hand of anyone who hefted it in battle,
> anyone who had fought and faced the worst
> in the gap of danger. This was not the first time
> it had been called to perform heroic feats.
>
> (1459–64)

Never had Hrunting failed; it was *not* the first time it had suc-
ceeded in the rush of battle. The poet leads his audience to
have faith in the sword's power. These details set the subsequent failure of the sword in deeper relief; and then, when the
sword unexpectedly *does* fail against Grendel's mother, what
the poet dwells upon is the unprecedented nature of this failure:

> But he [Beowulf] soon found
> his battle-torch extinguished: the shining blade
> refused to bite. It spared her and failed
> the man in his need. It had gone through many
> hand-to-hand fights, had hewed the armour
> and helmets of the doomed, but here at last
> the fabulous powers of that heirloom failed.
>
> (1522–28)

One immediate effect of the sword's failure is heightened suspense at this narrative moment, another turn of the screw:
just when things could not get worse, they do. But what the

poet especially devotes attention to is the defeat or reversal of expectations; the moment serves as a complex flashback—the unexpected failure gestures back to all the precedent moments of triumph in the sword's history.

The failure of swords is part of a pervasive narrative
pattern in the poem: the unexpected and unforeseen nul-
lification of commonsensical, established knowledge. For
example, the poet goes to some length to show us startling
exceptions to ethical conventions and assumptions. It is a
truism of the poem (and early medieval heroic convention)
that men will be loyal to their lord if rewarded and well-led.
And so, in the poem's prologue, we learn that the Danish
Beow (son of Scyld) was a model young leader, rewarding his
household men; the narrator approves and explains by precept that a leader should be generous and give freely so that
in his old age steadfast companions will stand by him and
serve him whenever war comes (20–24). This is the theory,
and in the second half of the poem, having been rewarded
generously by their king, it is therefore to be expected that
Beowulf's household warriors should support him bravely
in his final struggle—yet, defying expectations, they do not
do so, when put to the test and the dragon's fire (2631–60,
2845–91).

The poem undercuts many such assumptions. For example, it is a common-sense theory that women married off to
the right person should solve the problem of revenge; inter-
marriage should inhibit such strife by creating in-laws and
knitting people together. Yet in the world of the poem, its
tragic treatment of both Hildeburh and Freawaru argues that
this conventional theory, this precedent, will not work. Moreover, just as in-laws should not take up swords, the natural
expectation is that direct kin also should not (and will not) kill
each other. And so Wealtheow posits a future of peace and
amity for the next generation of Danish royalty (1179–86); but
the poem implies otherwise: a future of destructive kin-strife
(1014–18). Another assumption: it is to be expected that kings
govern their people according to respected ethical conventions: our poem shows us the exception in Heremod (1709–23).

Similarly, the customary role for queens is to provide a source of social/ethical stability: our poet shows us the exception in Modthryth/Fremu (1925–57), who defies the poem's ideal of queenly femininity, producing terror, not peace.

Furthermore, according to all accepted heroic conventions, a good warrior should be always ready for anything and will prosper if he follows that precept. Thus, although the Danish retainers asleep in Heorot after celebrations following the defeat of Grendel have little apparent reason for fear with the threat removed, nevertheless they are poised for action, as any good troop of warriors should be. The poet goes to some length to tell us that their shields, helmets, mail, and spears are all ready to hand as they prepare the hall for sleep "as so often in the past" (1238); it was their "habit" (1246) to be ready for war anywhere, at home or on the field of battle or anywhere need befell their prince (1248–50). Such prudence and readiness defines their good character: in the narrator's final approving summary, reflecting on their preparations: "[t]hey were a right people" (1250). However, all this preparation and admirable adherence to heroic readiness is for naught: although common sense tells them they have no monster left to fear (yet even so they are ready for action), their frame of expectation apparently cannot include the successful attack of Grendel's mother—another sudden unanticipated event that overturns all customary precautions.

In fact, armed retainers in the poem are often caught in that moment between expectation and unanticipated change. Beowulf's men *never* seem to predict accurately what will happen, even if their prediction is based on prior experience and common sense. For example, our hero himself is confident when he lays his head to rest in Heorot, waiting for Grendel; he delivers a final vow in which he resolves to fight Grendel barehanded, without weapons. However, as his men join him in sleep, the narrator pauses to tell us that they are not so optimistic:

> None of them expected he would ever see
> his homeland again or get back

> to his native place and the people who reared him.
> They knew too well the way it was before,
> how often the Danes had fallen prey
> to death in the mead-hall. (691–96)

The precedent is clear: death has carried off too many men for any reasonable person to expect that this night will be any different. And their leader wants to fight this creature without weapons? Yet, beyond expectation, this night *is* different: Beowulf triumphs and they *do* see their homes again (except Hondscioh).

Likewise, later in the poem, when Grendel's blood wells up out of the mere, the Danes leave in defeat; Beowulf's men cannot quite bring themselves to depart, but nevertheless they do not think their leader will come back:

> but sick at heart,
> staring at the mere, the strangers held on.
> They wished, without hope, to behold their lord,
> Beowulf himself. (1602–5; cf. also 1594–99)

They did not expect (*ne wendon*) to see him again. Yet, defying expectations, they do. The triumph of Beowulf's beheading of Grendel's body below is contrasted with the pessimism and dejection of the men above. In fact, a most wondrous unexpected event is happening below at that very moment—the giant sword blade is melting away like ice. This unexpected wonder below anticipates the marvel to come above when Beowulf breaks the surface of the water and returns.

Beowulf and the dragon both find things turn out very differently than they expect. The dragon has faith in something that has never failed him before: "now he felt secure / in the vaults of his barrow; but his trust was unavailing" (2322–23). We remember the dragon's misplaced confidence when, after the battle, the Geats look upon the wreck of the creature's once-soaring body; the poet allows a characteristic moment of reflection to enter his construction of the scene, as he contrasts the freedom and confidence of the dragon's flight with the earth-bound outcome of its death:

> He had shimmered forth
> on the night air once, then winged back
> down to his den; but death owned him now,
> he would never enter his earth-gallery again.
> (3043–46)

Similarly, Beowulf thinks an iron shield might provide better protection against the dragon's fire than a wooden one. However, this innovation does not work as well as expected, leading to an unprecedented defeat for the formerly invincible hero:

> Yet his shield defended
> the renowned leader's life and limb
> for a shorter time than he meant it to:
> that final day was the first time
> when Beowulf fought and fate denied him
> glory in battle. (2570–75)

The poet goes to some lengths to tell us that defeat was not something Beowulf himself could predict. Beowulf, a noble man who had always in the past proved tried and true (*æþeling ærgod*, 2342a), does not fear the dragon "for he had kept going / often in the past, through perils and ordeals / of every sort" (2349–51). The poet continually reemphasizes that Beowulf's undefeated past colours his failure in the present:

> And so the son of Ecgtheow had survived
> every extreme, excelling himself
> in daring and in danger, until the day arrived
> when he had to come face to face with the
> dragon. (2397–400)

What seems to fascinate the poet are these moments of punctuated novelty, when all the precedents fail to hold ground—a strange and original perspective, in a culture that values the predictability of tradition so highly. The poet thus creates a sense of constant newness, a notion that we are meant to marvel at the sequence of new, surprising, unprecedented events unfolding before us. Although these moments certainly serve to develop narrative suspense, their ubiquity in the poem's rhetorical architecture also lends them a cumulative philosophical significance as the poem progresses.

"Never before" and the Reversal of Fortune

These narrative movements of unprecedented change are further underwritten by a chorus of verbal patterns that emphasize the unprecedented nature of the action. Irving and others have noted the importance of *oððæt* ("until") as a narrative marker of turnabout in the poem.[4] Another pervasive tactic is the formulaic use of negative assertion: *næfre ... ær* ("never before") and related expressions. The narrator tells us, for example, that he has *not* heard of a ship more gloriously laden with treasure than Scyld's death ship (38–40); he has *never* heard of a company of people gathering together in better amity and decorum than the Danes (1010–11); and he has *not* heard of a better necklace than the one Hrothgar presents to Beowulf since Hama carried away the torque of the Brosings (1197–1201). Reacting to Beowulf's farewell, Hrothgar notes that he has *never* heard such a young man speak so wisely (1842–43). In his report to Hygelac, Beowulf tells the assembled Geat court that in Denmark he had *never* seen anywhere under the heavens a happier people (2014–16). When he challenges Beowulf and his men, the Danish coast guard says that an armed company has *never* approached Hrothgar's realm so brashly, and *never* has he seen a more impressive sight than their leader (244–49); Wulfgar, the hall-guard of Heorot, echoes the trope, declaring that he has *never* seen so many strangers arrive in such a bold fashion (337–38); and on the eve of Beowulf's fight with Grendel, Hrothgar tells his court that he has *never* handed keeping of Heorot over to any other man. Deeding such responsibility to a stranger—or any-

---

4 For example, at lines 99–101. See Irving, *A Reading of* Beowulf (New Haven: Yale University Press, 1968), 31–42; T. A. Shippey, *Old English Verse* (London: Hutchinson, 1972), 38; Lapidge, "*Beowulf* and Perception," 63–64.

one—is an unprecedented act, as Hrothgar himself makes clear: "Never, since my hand could hold a shield / have I entrusted or given control / of the Danes' hall to anyone but you" (655–57). These repeated uses of "never/*næfre*" have a cumulative effect—they embellish the poem's narrative patterns of defeated expectations and progressively generate an unusual pervasive atmosphere of novelty and highlight the contingent nature of human affairs.

The narrator even expresses the monsters' experience in the same way. For example, as Grendel approaches Heorot to meet his doom, the poet tells us that it was *not* the first time the monster had sought the hall; thus, he has the "expectation of an extensive feast" (*wistfylle wen*, 734a), and why should his expectation be any different this time? As the narrator tells us,

> Nor was that the first time
> he had scouted the grounds of Hrothgar's dwelling—
> although *never* in his life, before or since,
> did he find harder fortune or hall-defenders.
> (716–19)

When he reaches for his customary victim/meal and instead finds Beowulf's grasp, this celebrated moment pauses to reflect on this unprecedented reversal:

> The captain of evil discovered himself
> in a handgrip harder than anything
> he had ever encountered in any man
> on the face of the earth. Every bone in his body
> quailed and recoiled, but he could not escape.
> (749–53)

Grendel is desperate to flee to his home, because, as the poet summarizes, dwelling even further upon the moment: "for in all his days / he had *never* been clamped or cornered like this" (755–56).

The poet also tells us that the Danes marvelled that the hall withstood the violent forces inside it:

> The story goes
> that as the pair struggled, mead-benches were smashed
> and sprung off the floor, gold fittings and all.
> Before then, no Shielding elder would believe
> there was any power or person upon earth
> capable of wrecking their horn-rigged hall
> unless the burning embrace of a fire
> engulf it in flame. (774–81)

The emphasis on contingency generated by these *never*-patterns intensifies and unites the other disparate unexpected/ unprecedented events that occur at different points in the narrative. Therefore, as the experience of the poem unfolds in time for reader or auditor, the constant interplay of contingency and causality conditions the meaning of the poem's narrative for the human lives caught up in those events. From this perspective, human decisions seem both more and less important, at the same time, as the broader defining context of historical change circumscribes the characters' lives and stories.

As if to punctuate this pervasive rhetoric of novelty, the rare nouns *edwenden* and *edhwyrft* (both meaning "turnabout" or "change in fortune") occur at important narrative moments. Beowulf explains to the coast-guard that Hrothgar must accept Beowulf's help if the king is ever to find *edwenden* (277–85, at 280a). The narrator describes the sudden attack of Grendel's mother upon the sleeping Danes as an *edhwyrft* (1279–82, at 1281a). In his central speech upon contemplation of the giant sword-hilt from Grendel's lair, Hrothgar explains how he ruled the Danes joyfully for fifty years, until Grendel suddenly brought *edwenden* upon him in his hall (1774–78, at 1774b).

Finally, Beowulf returns home and the narrator tells us, in a lingering framed moment of pause and transition, that his great deeds have brought him *edwenden* in his life:

> Thus Beowulf bore himself with valour;
> he was formidable in battle yet behaved with honour
> and took no advantage; never cut down
> a comrade who was drunk, kept his temper
> and, warrior that he was, watched and controlled

his God-sent strength and his outstanding
natural powers. He had been poorly regarded
for a long time, was taken by the Geats
for less than he was worth: and their lord too
had never much esteemed him in the mead-hall.
They firmly believed that he lacked force,
that the prince was a weakling; but presently
every affront to his deserving was reversed [*edwenden*].
(2177-89)

A few lines later the scene will suddenly shift to Beowulf fifty years later, an old man ready for his last battle, while the word *edwenden* is still echoing in our minds. At this point, the transition from the first part of the poem to the second part (2200-10), which leaves out all the tumultuous events that led to Beowulf's assumption of the throne, is itself sudden and unexpected, a narrative *edwenden* for the reader. We later learn, through flashback, the detailed events that led to Beowulf's (unexpected) kingship, but the transition here highlights the crossroads, when Beowulf's life went one way, and not another.

Humanist Ramifications of Contingency

However, it is not simply that "unexpected things" happen in the poem—that could be an element of any narrative with any sort of plot or suspense. Rather, part of our poet's narrative sensibility is to frame these unprecedented changes in various ways, dwelling upon the pause of events as they heave to and change direction. In these pauses, the poem enables a subtle and complex view of human character. For example, when Hrothgar learns of the new attack from Grendel's mother, Beowulf is summoned and the poem gives us a studied and moving turning-point passage, a moment of paused transition:

And the old lord,
the grey-haired warrior, was heartsore and weary
when he heard the news: his highest-placed adviser,
his dearest companion, was dead and gone.

> Beowulf was quickly brought to the chamber:
> the winner of fights, the arch-warrior,
> came first-footing in with his fellow troops
> to where the king in his wisdom waited,
> still wondering whether Almighty God
> would ever turn the tide of his misfortunes. (1306–15)

Using simultaneous points of view, the poet highlights the contrast between Beowulf and Hrothgar at this moment: as he strides to the summons, Beowulf is content in his victory belonging to the world before the unexpected appearance of Grendel's mother; but waiting on the other side of that divide Hrothgar is tormented in mind, knowing that a new threat has appeared. By juxtaposing the inner mental states of two characters linked in a moment of pregnant pause, the poet dramatizes the effect of contingency in the world at the level of human lives.

In these moments of pause and dilation, the poet shows his characters brooding upon the sudden changes in the world around them; in this way he makes concrete and particular the more abstract movements, puzzles, ironies, and enigmas of history and causality.[5] In order to make experience concrete and to explore the human condition, the poet ponders individuals and how they react to unprecedented changes. Hrothgar ponders his lot with personal sorrow during Grendel's reign, again when he gazes upon Grendel's arm fixed on high, and most famously, after he looks upon the giant sword hilt. Hygelac feels the surge of emotion about his heart when Beowulf suddenly departs for Denmark, fearing the outcome (1992–98). Hengest and the Last Survivor both meditate upon the world and its random ways (1128–41, 2236b–70a). Beowulf experiences this same emotion surging up upon the sudden attack of the dragon and the news of his home's destruction (2327–33).

---

[5] For an elegant essay on the poem's representation of history see Roberta Frank, "The *Beowulf* Poet's Sense of History" (1982); repr. in NCE, 168–82.

We find this sad evocation of the individual life placed against the force of events in one of the narrator's summary comments upon Beowulf's death:

> Famous for his deeds
> a warrior may be, but it remains a mystery
> where his life will end, when he may no longer
> dwell in the mead-hall among his own.
> So it was with Beowulf, when he faced the cruelty
> and cunning of the mound-guard. He himself was ignorant
> of how his departure from the world would happen. (3062–68)

In all of these cases, events take a changing path few might have expected or predicted; the poet presents the human significance of these actions. Moreover, as it constructs these narrative reflections, the narrator's voice is not always clearly consistent in intent; these moments of narrative pause are not simply or uniformly expressed as "transience" or "mutability," or consistently presented throughout the poem in accordance with any obvious dogma. What we can say is this: the poet finds his depth in the moments of pause, when the past feeds the present and opens up to the future. Something in the way the narrator presents these scenes, shuttling back and forth between enigmatic objectivity and hortatory comment, creates a complex narrative effect, a rich and subtle emotional response that we do not explain adequately if we simply label it "fatalistic" or "elegiac" or an expression of the traditional *lif biþ læne* ("life is transitory") theme. The poet is peculiarly interested in placing the reader in these moments of pause in which "a disconfirmation [is] followed by a consonance."[6] As Kermode further explains, the "end comes as expected, but not in the manner expected."[7] This dialectic makes *Beowulf* an intellectually demanding, "participatory" poem, requiring much from its readers.

---

6 Kermode, *Sense of an Ending*, 18.

7 Kermode, *Sense of an Ending*, 53.

Wyrd and Contingency

But does the poem ever address the ultimate questions behind emergent occasions? That is, who or what is behind these events? Is there a hand on the rudder of the world? Or is the ship simply drifting on the currents? As always, the multiple voices of the poem provide multiple answers. The narrator tends to place God behind events: for example, "The truth is clear: / Almighty God rules over mankind / and always has" (700–702); as Beowulf awaits Grendel in Heorot, the narrator assures us that the "King of Glory / ... had posted a lookout / who was a match for Grendel" (665–67); when Beowulf wrestles Grendel's mother, the narrator tells us that "holy God / decided the victory" for Beowulf (1553–54). Hrothgar, Beowulf, and even Wiglaf at times invoke God's power in a similar way. When Beowulf arrives at Heorot, Hrothgar declares that "Now Holy God / has, in His goodness, guided him here / to the West-Danes" (381–83); when he sees Grendel's gory trophy-arm, he gives thanks to "the Almighty Father / ... for this sight"; declares also that "the Heavenly Shepherd / can work his wonders always and everywhere"; and that Beowulf has accomplished his victory "with the Lord's assistance" (927–30, 939). After his successful battle in Grendel's home, Beowulf tells Hrothgar and the others that "God ... helped" him, and that "the Lord of Men allowed [him] to behold" the ancient giant sword on the wall because "[God] often helps the unbefriended" (1661–63).

But sometimes the animating force behind events is described in other ways, as the workings of *wyrd*, or similar locutions for "fate, destiny." *Wyrd* (a noun that derives from the Old English verb *weorðan*, "to become") can have a variety of meanings in Old English: *wyrd* can simply mean "events" or "things that happen" all the way up to a more formalized concept, almost a personification, as "Fate" or "Destiny."[8] The narrator tells us that when Hygelac died,

---

8 For bibliography on *wyrd* see the word's glossary entry in Klaeber. Two good essays on the complexities of *wyrd* in the poem: Mary C. Wilson Tietjen, "God, Fate, and the Hero of *Beowulf*," *JEGP* 74 (1975):

"fate [*wyrd*] swept him away" (1205); when Beowulf's men sleep in Heorot, unaware that Grendel's mother was coming for revenge, the narrator asks "how could they know fate [*wyrd*], / the grim shape of things to come"? (1233–4). Grendel enters Heorot to fight Beowulf, but even after all the narrator's assertions that God determined the outcome, the narrative voice still says (about Grendel): "his fate [*wyrd*] that night / was due to change, his days of ravening / had come to an end" (733–35). Just prior to facing the dragon, Beowulf reflects on his life, and the narrator comments:

> He was sad at heart,
> unsettled yet ready, sensing his death.
> His fate [*wyrd*] hovered near, unknowable but certain:
> it would soon claim his coffered soul,
> part life from limb. Before long
> the prince's spirit would spin free from his body. (2419–24)

Beowulf also speaks of *wyrd*, even though he also speaks of God. For example, even in his first speech to Hrothgar he attributes the outcome of events to God ("Whichever one death fells / must deem it a just judgement by God" [440–41]), but then finishes the speech a few lines later by attributing the same outcomes to *wyrd*: "Fate [*wyrd*] goes ever as fate must" (455). His final words to his thanes before they await Grendel in Heorot give God the power to direct events: "And may the Divine Lord / in His wisdom grant the glory of victory / to whichever side He sees fit" (685–87); but prior to this, in his recounting of the swimming match with Breca, and his own survival, he summarizes: "Often, for undaunted courage, / fate [*wyrd*] spares the man it has not already marked" (572–73).

It can be difficult to know whether any given instance of *wyrd* simply means "events" or something more formalized and personified. Moreover, fate/*wyrd* and God need not be opposed: medieval theology resolved the two within a Christian framework, as God's Providence. Scholars have tried to

159–71; Jon C. Kasik, "The Use of the Term 'Wyrd' in *Beowulf* and the Conversion of the Anglo-Saxons," *Neophilologus* 63 (1979): 128–35.

come up with an explanation that might organize and clarify all these possible contradictions, but the truth is that the voices and perspectives are too varied; whether this is the poet's intention or a discordant effect of the poem's evolution does not in the end matter. What is clear is this: the poem could have simply and universally ascribed everything, all events in the poem, to the power of God, Jesus, the Trinity and expunged all other possibilities. The poem also could have clearly and explicitly invoked the devil as the source of evil and misery and misfortune in the world, as in many other Old English works. *Beowulf* is a poem, a world of verbal art, and not a theological or philosophical treatise making a formal argument; poetry tends to express ideas in complex and ambiguous ways, and *Beowulf*'s existential meditations are not reducible to a simple theological formula.

The poem therefore raises questions about the human story, but does not provide us with clear definitive answers; that is, in fact, part of the poem's humanist project—to elaborate a sharp, clearly felt view of human lives in history, a view that in the end resists full assimilation to any one sentiment, dogma, or religious system of any sort. The poet's construction of human character through these artful ambiguities destabilizes any systematic apprehension of humanity's place in the world; instead, the poet creates an innovative *narrative* construction and apprehension of character. In its meditations upon the emergent occasion, "unprevented for all our diligence, unsuspected for all our curiosity,"[9] *Beowulf* dramatizes the changing shape of human lives in response to contingent circumstances. The poet shows us humanity in time, *homo historicus*, the political animal caught in the entropy of time and change. In the end, when the complex voices in *Beowulf* are weighed one against the other, the varied pronouncements of our narrator against the overall action and its final ambiguities, we find that this most puzzling and unexpected of poems offers no easy answers—only a stark, enigmatic view of time, history, and change.

---

9 Donne, *Devotions Upon Emergent Occasions*, 7.

Chapter 3

Tragedy

Let us recap where we have come so far in my claim that *Beowulf* is a moving work of art, to be read and admired because it is a profoundly humanist poem. In Chapter 1, I asserted that doubt permeates *Beowulf*; and doubt is an essential element of any humanist enterprise. Chapter 2 showed that the poem is also fascinated by the contingent aspect of human events, a logical complement to doubt. Chapter 3 now takes us one step further: if the poem represents the human presence as defined by doubt in the face of emergent occasions, how does the poem then more deeply try to understand that dilemma? The answer is: as tragedy.

"Tragedy" is a notoriously complex and fraught term in literary study, but let me summarize here my view of *Beowulf* as humanist tragedy in the pages to come. The contingent nature of events reveals a basic humanist problem: the prospect that human beings exist, and often suffer, on their own in an unjust and capricious world. *Beowulf* expresses this dilemma through the literary mode we have come to call tragedy; tragedy represents the human presence suffering at the epicentre of large, contending impersonal forces. There have been many critical readings of the poem focused on Beowulf or Hrothgar or other characters as tragic, but a certain line of criticism has seen the tragic vision of the poem as embodied in the female characters, and I develop that tradition here.[1] I am not arguing that the poem is exclusively tragic; Chapter 4 will move us in a somewhat different direction. Also, this is not an argument about genre: I am not saying the poem should be "classified" as a tragedy. *Beowulf* is too heterogenous a composition to submit to any one label.[2] *Beowulf* is a humanist poem in that it deploys the mode of tragedy strategically, in carefully focused ways, as part of its multiple attempts to understand the human story.

So, this chapter will focus on tragedy and the women of *Beowulf*.[3] Casual readers sometimes knock *Beowulf* for its lack of "central" or "strong" female character, but one cannot judge importance in a work of art simply by measuring the length of roles. There are, in fact, many female characters in *Beowulf*; the poet has selected and developed female characters in careful ways that are lost if *Beowulf* becomes (once again) nothing more than "Beowulf, Monster-Slayer." It is very easy to imagine a *Beowulf* truly bereft of women: just read a

---

1 See, e.g., Martin Camargo, "The Finn Episode and the Tragedy of Revenge in 'Beowulf'," *Studies in Philology* 78.5 (1981): 120–134.

2 See Joseph Harris, "*Beowulf* in Literary History" (1982) repr. in *Interpretations of* Beowulf, ed. Fulk, 235–41, for a study of the poem's generic diversity, arguing that is almost an anthology of ancient Germanic literary genres.

3 There have been many fine analyses of women and gender in *Beowulf*; for an overview see Alexandra Hennessey Olsen, "Gender Roles," in *A Beowulf Handbook*, ed. Bjork and Niles, 311–24. I have been influenced by all the scholars cited in this chapter, as well as the following: Jane Chance, "The Structural Unity of *Beowulf*: The Problem of Grendel's Mother" (1980); repr. in NCE, 153–168, and her *Woman as Hero in Old English Literature* (Syracuse: Syracuse University Press, 1986); Clare A. Lees, "Men and *Beowulf*" (1994), repr. in *The Postmodern* Beowulf: *A Critical Casebook*, ed. Eileen A. Joy and Mary K. Ramsey (Morgantown: West Virginia University Press, 2006), 418–38; Shari Horner, "Voices from the Margin: Women and Textual Enclosure in *Beowulf*" (2001), repr. in *The Postmodern* Beowulf, ed. Joy and Ramsey, 467–500; Stacy S. Klein, *Ruling Women: Queenship and Gender in Anglo-Saxon Literature* (Notre Dame: University of Notre Dame Press, 2006), 87–123.

poem like *The Battle of Maldon* or *The Battle of Brunanburh* or *The Song of Roland*. If *Beowulf* were truly *only* about men drinking and fighting and killing, there would be no need or room for Wealhtheow, Hildeburh, Freawaru, Hygd, Thryth/ Fremu, Grendel's mother, and so forth; no reason to include women in *any* fashion. It is easy to imagine such a version of the *Beowulf* narrative re-imagined in a far more exclusively masculinist way: cut the women and instead describe some of Hrothgar's early battles; more dialogue and scenes of Hroth-gar consulting with his men over the Grendel threat; a wise old counsellor substituting for Wealhtheow; perhaps a scene of Hrothgar's men battling Grendel, only to be defeated; cut Grendel's mother and give him a grim and terrible father instead; show us more of Beowulf's youth, including a scene with his father; devote more space to Hygelac's disastrous Frisian raid; extended scenes of fighting, like Wulf and Eofor's slaying of Ongentheow. Perhaps a strong son for Beowulf, as a companion to Wiglaf? Why not extended scenes of mov-ing deaths of retainers by their lord's side, as in *Maldon*? The more well-read one is in *Beowulf*'s Germanic sources and analogues, and the more immersed one is in general with classical and early medieval literary options, the clearer it is what the *Beowulf*-poet could have done, but chose not to do.

In short, like other artistic options at the poet's hand, the women of the poem have been carefully chosen and pre-sented for particular ends and effects. That end is tragedy. As Gillian Overing (one of the most sophisticated readers of the poem's gender dynamics) explains, the women of Beowulf are ambiguous disruptors of order in the poem, "hysterics," as she terms them; they are agents of potential or actual disturbance to the dominant masculine heroic ethos of the poem, an integral counterpoint to the work's masculinist voices.[4] In order to compose a proudly humanist meditation, the poet has, in a subtle fashion, engaged the women as a

---

4 Gillian Overing, *Language, Sign, and Gender in Beowulf* (Carbondale: Southern Illinois University Press, 1990). She condensed many of her book's conclusions into the essay "The Women of *Beowulf*:

way to explore a tragic vision of the human story. Women in the poem stand for the human presence at its most poignant. This chapter will first say a few words about how I am using the amorphous term "tragedy"; then survey most of these female characters to explicate this tragic pattern.

Tragedy and Humanism

Beowulf has been called a tragedy or tragic by many, usually in a loose sense.[5] Scholars often recognize the weakness of Hrothgar and the death of Beowulf as "tragic" in some capacity, and the tribal conflicts woven into the second half of the poem as also "tragic," though there is not complete agreement on either of these assertions. There is no influence of classical tragic drama on the poem, either directly or through intermediaries; so, if we speak of anything in the poem as "tragic," it is "tragedy" used in a transhistorical literary sense.[6]

Given this, I would focus on two fundamental elements of tragedy. First, tragedy is about endings, a commonplace of tragic theory: "The basis of the tragic vision," as Northrop Frye puts it, "is being in time."[7] By this Frye means that tragedy springs from the human dilemma of being finite creatures existing and struggling in a world of finite time. We are all born, live out our lives, and then die: "Death is what defines the individual, and marks him off from the continuity of life that flows indefinitely between the past and the future"; or, as Eagleton

---

A Context for Interpretation" (2000) in *The* Beowulf *Reader*, ed. Baker, 219–60; it is from this essay that I cite.

5 For discussion of how *Beowulf* might be classified as tragedy see Stanley B. Greenfield, "*Beowulf* and Epic Tragedy" (1962), repr. in *Hero and Exile*, 1–17.

6 For an overview of tragedy as a transhistorical literary mode see the history by Terry Eagleton, *Sweet Violence: The Idea of the Tragic* (Oxford: Blackwell, 2003); and Adrian Poole, *Tragedy: Shakespeare and the Greek Example* (Oxford: Blackwell, 1987).

7 Northrop Frye, *Fools of Time: Studies in Shakespearean Tragedy* (Toronto: University of Toronto Press, 1967), 3.

notes, tragedy "can be among other things a symbolic coming to terms with our finitude and fragility."[8] This human predicament of being creatures subject to time links tragedy with the contingency of events. It is demarcation—separating one chain of events, provisionally, from another—that gives retroactive shape to that narrative and shapes the possibilities of the future. That process of demarcating a sequence of events constitutes the finality of tragedy. Taken as a whole, *Beowulf* is far more often about endings than about beginnings, a meditation on death rather than on life. *Beowulf* is not the bright world of comedy or romance: marriages tend to fail, rather than produce a new generation; burials, tombs, and funerals tend to dominate the action, not dances, cakes, and ale; the old have borne too much and lived too long; characters do not wander unpathed waters and undreamed shores in search of home, but rather unexpected horror erupts in their own home; instead of a green world of fecund transformation, we see the wasteland and the haunted barrow.[9]

Second, tragedy is about suffering; not always or only about a central hero's suffering, but rather in Eagleton's words, tragedy is about the formation of a "community of suffering."[10] Why and how we find pleasure in the depiction of suffering is beyond my purposes here. But an important part of the theory of tragic suffering, and how it pertains to *Beowulf*, is that tragic art is a remembrance of suffering, a commemoration that paradoxically conjures up both sorrow and joy, as Poole argues:

> Tragedy's medicine for misery consists not in a kind of forgetting but in a kind of remembering, a commemoration of suffering through which human grief is at one and the same time relived and relieved. But, further and finally, it

---

8 Frye, *Fools of Time*, 3; Eagleton, *Sweet Violence*, xv.

9 On the funerals in *Beowulf* see Gale R. Owen-Crocker, *The Four Funerals in Beowulf and the Structure of the Poem* (Manchester: Manchester University Press, 2000).

10 Eagleton, *Sweet Violence*, xvi.

is a commemoration not only of suffering but also of joy, neither one without the other. ... [Tragedy] embodies our most paradoxical feelings and thoughts and beliefs. It gives them flesh and blood, emotional and intellectual and spiritual substance. Through tragedy we recognize and refill our sense of both the value and the futility of human life, of both its purposes and its emptiness.[11]

As tragic art, *Beowulf* is about endings; it also bears witness to and commemorates "the value and futility of human life." Let us examine how the women of *Beowulf* fit into this understanding of tragedy and its memories.

Freawaru

The consequences of retaliatory violence are a central part of how tragedy works in *Beowulf*. We do not want a modern anti-violence perspective to lead to a misunderstanding of vendettas in the poem. Violence was not only an accepted part of life, but was indeed a positive opportunity for the testing of courage and honour; a way to achieve glory and reputation; sometimes a way, paradoxically, to settle disputes with finality rather than perpetuate them.[12] However, it would also be a mistake to say that no one saw the tragic costs of violence. To speak of the "tragedy" of revenge or ambivalence toward violence, as I will in this chapter, is not anachronistic, not a case of imparting a modern distaste for violence. Yes, at one point Beowulf declares: "It is always better / to avenge dear ones than to indulge in mourning" (1384–85); i.e., active vengeance is honorable. But such a sentiment is not the only perspective in the poem; there are other voices to be heard.

Take the episode of Freawaru and Ingeld (lines 2020–69). This is a tale told by Beowulf to Hygelac and the Geat court

---

11 Poole, *Tragedy: Shakespeare and the Greek Example*, 239.

12 See John M. Hill's *The Cultural World in* Beowulf (Toronto: University of Toronto Press, 1995) and Peter Baker, *Honour, Exchange and Violence in* Beowulf (Cambridge: Brewer, 2013).

upon his return home after his adventures in Denmark. In the course of his account, Beowulf notes that the Danish court included Hrothgar's daughter Freawaru, a "young bride-to-be / to the gracious Ingeld" (2024–25) who will, hopefully, cement bonds between the two peoples. Ingeld, king of the Heatho-bards, is a figure familiar from Germanic legend, as was his grudge against Hrothgar and the Danes, a history of violence that would eventually result in the destruction of Heorot itself. So, there is an unusual game here with the audience's expec-tations. Beowulf goes on in this episode to predict the failure of Freawaru and Ingeld's marriage; he vividly postulates and imagines what to him and to the people around him is some-thing that *might* happen in the future, but from the latter-day early medieval audience perspective (familiar with the ancient legend) has *already* happened long ago in the legendary past: the uneasy peace between Danes and Heathobards will fail. From the perspective of the characters in the poem, this pos-sibility is presented as just that: a possible, but likely, future event. However, since the audience of the poem knew the overall shape of the story, we know that what Beowulf narrates as an imagined *possible* outcome is indeed the *inevitable* out-come. Why these ironies? Remember that tragedy is a remem-brance and commemoration of suffering: the *Beowulf*-poet sets up Freawaru's tragedy in this complex way so that for the reader the episode is a studied act of remembrance, brought to memory and commemorated by the community. "Com-memorated" here in two senses: remembered by a group and also honoured and distinguished as a special act of intellection.

This story was available to the poet in oral tradition, as raw material to be shaped in any number of possible ways, but the poem chooses to design the episode using Freawaru as a focus. The episode is introduced through Freawaru: Beowulf first narrates her appearance and situation and then conjures up a vivid future scene: Ingeld shall walk into his own hall with Freawaru at his side, with Danish guests in her retinue, mingling with their erstwhile enemies. However, the Danes attending their princess openly wear trophies that at one time they stripped from dead Heathobards on the battlefield. A trouble-making old warrior who *remembers* every-thing shall point out to a young Heathobard warrior (to Ingeld himself in some analogues) his deceased father's sword on the hip of a hated Dane. Violence awakens as the young war-rior kills the Dane to avenge his father, Freawaru falling into focus as the vendetta re-awakens:

> "And so he [the old warrior] keeps on, recalling and accusing,
> working things up with bitter words
> until one of the lady's retainers lies
> spattered in blood, split open
> on his father's account." (2057–61)

Beowulf narrates the flight of the killer, the demand for retal-iation, and he ends the episode as it began, with a final focus on Freawaru:

> "... a passionate hate
> will build up in Ingeld, and love for his bride
> will falter in him as the feud rankles." (2064–66)

There is plenty of mental and physical suffering to go around here: the old warrior's grudge; the shame and anger of the young warrior; the failure of Ingeld and Freawaru's love; the ruin of the marriage and the political union it represents; a bloody murder in a hall. The poem is notably silent about Freawaru's thoughts at the end of the episode, leaving her situation and thoughts powerfully understated.

Hygd

We see the same tragic pattern when we turn to Hygelac's queen, Hygd. The poet first introduces us to Hygd upon Beowulf's return home. Hygelac has been mentioned regu-larly by Beowulf in the poem; when we finally "meet" the king in the narrative, we also meet his wife Hygd: the poet's first detail about her is that she is young, and the court around her a youthful community at the apex of its happiness and promise:

> The building was magnificent, the king majestic,
> ensconced in his hall; and although Hygd, his queen,
> was young, a few short years at court,
> her mind was thoughtful and her manners sure.
> Haereth's daughter behaved generously
> and stinted nothing when she distributed
> bounty to the Geats. (1925-31)

Hygd and the young court are clearly meant to call to mind
Hrothgar's similar young company from the beginning of the
poem (lines 64-85). Beowulf presents Hygd with the fabu-
lous necklace given to him by Hrothgar; it is compared to a
mythic torque of Germanic legend. The poet then notes that
this very necklace would be also on Hygelac's breast when
he dies too young, linking the two characters, dead king and
his wife. After Hygelac's death, Hygd is put in a tough place.
With surrounding enemies on the march upon her husband's
death, the Geat kingdom must be protected. Should the
throne go to their young son Heardred? She has her doubts
and instead offers the throne to Beowulf:

> There Hygd offered him throne and authority
> as lord of the ring-hoard: with Hygelac dead,
> she had no belief in her son's ability
> to defend their homeland against foreign invaders.
>
> (2369-72)

Beowulf nevertheless declines this offer, a well-meaning decision that turns out to have tragic consequences: eventually
it brings about her son Heardred's death, as he makes the
foolish mistake of sheltering the Swedish princes Eanmund
and Eadgils, young exiles on the run from their usurping
uncle Onela. Onela kills Heardred, leaving Beowulf as king;
Beowulf, in turn, eventually avenges Heardred. But the poem
passes over any further mention of Hygd—a telling silence,
once again implying her plight rather than detailing it. And
so our poem's camera eye sees her twice: once in the flush
of beauty and youth and optimism; and once in desperate
straits, caught in the midst of unexpected events that will
make her lose her son just as she has lost her husband. We

are not given her words or her inner thoughts or any note of her in the aftermath—a telling silence.

Wealhtheow

A similar tragic pattern envelops Wealhtheow. Of the female characters, she is given the largest direct presence in the poem, as has long been recognized.[13] The queen enters the poem in stately fashion; we learn that she, like Freawaru, might have been married to Hrothgar from another tribe: she is a "Helming woman." She offers a ceremonial cup to Beowulf:

> With measured words she welcomed the Geat
> and thanked God for granting her wish
> that a deliverer she could believe in would arrive
> to ease their afflictions. (625–28)

What is unstated is important here. Beowulf has just put Unferth in his place, in the process also mocked the courage of the Danes and their inability to kill Grendel. Beowulf is the most vibrant man in Heorot now, an unstated rival to the other men: Unferth, Hrothgar himself, his son(s) with Wealhtheow, and Hrothulf (the king's nephew). The presence of this impressive Geat initiates subtle political dynamics centred around Wealhtheow.

After Beowulf kills Grendel, Hrothgar is overwhelmed with gratitude, and in what seems an odd emphasis, even praises the (unnamed) mother of Beowulf and "adopts" Beowulf as a son:

---

13 For an exhaustive study of Wealhtheow see Helen Damico, Beowulf's *Wealhtheow and the Valkyrie Tradition* (Madison: University of Wisconsin Press, 1984). A good recent survey of approaches to the character is Helen Conrad O'Briain, "Listening to the Woman: Reading Wealhtheow as Stateswoman," in *New Readings on Women and Early English Medieval Literature and Culture: Cross-Disciplinary Studies in Honour of Helen Damico*, ed. Helene Scheck and Christine E. Kozikowski (Leeds: Arc Humanities Press, 2019), 191–208.

> "Whoever she was
> who brought forth this flower of manhood,
> if she is still alive, that woman can say
> that in her labour the Lord of Ages
> bestowed a grace on her. So now, Beowulf,
> I adopt you in my heart as a dear son.
> Nourish and maintain this new connection,
> you noblest of men; there'll be nothing you'll want for,
> no worldly goods that won't be yours." (941–49)

Why not, at this moment, praise Beowulf's father? "With your courage and strength, O Beowulf, you have brought glory to the memory of your father, Ecgtheow. I thank the Lord he brought you into this world!" That sounds like something the poem could easily say; the point of mentioning his mother, rather, is to highlight the subtle dynamics involving women as this scene unfolds.

Hrothgar's words should alarm Wealhtheow for at least three reasons. First, Hrothgar has praised the child-bearing prowess of another woman, who produced a son that saved his kingdom—with his own child-bearing wife standing right there. Second, Hrothgar has promised Beowulf any material reward he wants. No limits? Third, and most alarming, he has "adopted" Beowulf as a son, when his own sons are sitting nearby. Not a formal, "real" adoption (one supposes), but even saying such a thing as a public courtesy is potentially dangerous. The queen must address the situation.

A bit later, after the tale of Hildeburh's tragedy, the poet finally gets to Wealhtheow's reply, first setting her down among the men in an emblematic fashion:

> ... Wealhtheow came to sit
> in her gold crown between two good men,
> uncle and nephew, each one of whom
> still trusted the other; and the forthright Unferth,
> admired by all for his mind and courage
> although under a cloud for killing his brothers,
> reclined near the king. (1161–67)

The poem's analogues tell us that this is not an innocent seating arrangement: the poem's audience would have known of the famous deadly rift eventually to come between "uncle and nephew," that is, between Hrothgar and Hrothulf. Hrothulf would one day take the throne from Hrothgar's son and kill him (see also lines 1014–18). The key word in this passage is "still" in "still trusted" (*þa gyt*, "then yet/still"), probably implying that *at that time*, there was still peace, but the inevitable strife between them was yet to come. Moreover, the details about Unferth and his kin-slaying, noted casually in passing, do not lend a note of optimism to the scene. The audience knows that Wealhtheow is surrounded by kin-slaying men, on the brink of a world of tragedy.

The queen then speaks to Hrothgar, carefully trying to negotiate the politics of the developing situation; she encourages the king to enjoy their deliverance, but cautions him:

> "The bright court of Heorot has been cleansed
> and now the word is that you want to adopt
> this warrior as a son. So, while you may,
> bask in your fortune, and then bequeath
> kingdom and nation to your kith and kin,
> before your decease. I am certain of Hrothulf.
> He is noble and will use the young ones well.
> He will not let you down. Should you die before him,
> he will treat our children truly and fairly.
> He will honour, I am sure, our two sons,
> repay them in kind when he recollects
> all the good things we gave him once,
> the favour and respect he found in his childhood."
>
> (1174–86)

"I am certain of Hrothulf"—a sad and ironic line. The point, of course, is that Hrothulf will very much *not* honour their children; just as in the well-known tragic tale of Freawaru and Ingeld, the audience knows that Hrothgar and Hrothulf will have a deadly falling-out: it is already a fact of legendary history, its retelling here a commemoration of tragic suffering.

The irony of this moment is complex. Wealhtheow is concerned that Hrothgar's too-eager esteem for this young stranger might upset the delicate balance in her family and her plans for the future. But we, the audience, know that her worries about Beowulf are misplaced: he is a good man, and when later in life in his own family he is faced with Hrothulf's exact choice, the Geat supports and protects his own young nephew. Beowulf is (or would not be) a threat to the Danes, even if he were to be taken into Hrothgar's household. On the other hand, her faith in Hrothulf is tragically misplaced: he *will* kill her children when the choice comes. In fact, if Hrothgar had adopted Beowulf as a "son," (unlikely as that might seem) the tragic suffering to come in her family might *not* have happened. Tragedy is often about the roads not taken, once again the contingent nature of events: what if the handkerchief had not dropped in *Othello*? What if Beowulf had been adopted into Hrothgar's household? We, the audience, knowing what we know about the unexpected course of later events, watch Wealhtheow at this moment make the wrong choice for the right reasons, and set in motion a chain of tragic events.

The scene ends by focusing on Wealhtheow again, just as it began with her, the woman in significantly silent tableau among the men:

> She turned then to the bench where her boys sat,
> Hrethric and Hrothmund, with other nobles' sons,
> all the youth together; and that good man,
> Beowulf the Geat, sat between the brothers.
> (1187–90)

It is typical of the poem's overall method that this moment of tableau says so much by implication and ambiguous suggestion. It is a moment of tragic pause, suggesting all the events that led to this moment and all the paths leading away from it into the future.

Hildeburh

The Hildeburh episode displays the same tragic pattern. It is placed at an important point in the poem: after Beowulf's victory over Grendel, there are celebrations in the hall and the court poet (*scop*) recites the legendary story of Hilde-burh: a Danish princess's tragic marriage to Finn, lord of the Frisians. The story of Hildeburh is much like the story of Freawaru: a princess is sent in marriage to another tribe. She marries Finn and bears his son. Her brother, the Dan-ish king Hnaef, visits his sister with a Danish retinue, includ-ing his man Hengest. During the visit, violence breaks out in Finn's hall. Hnaef is killed, along with Hildeburh's son by Finn, but the Danes following him defend the hall and force a stalemate. An ill-fated truce is drawn up: the surviving Danes (now lordless) will swear allegiance to Finn; Finn takes them as his men and promises to treat them as well as his own Frisians. The Danes would have preferred to die honorable deaths after Hnaef's fall, but Finn and the Frisians lack the manpower to finish them off. Hengest agrees and settles down for a brooding winter with his one-time deadly ene-mies, who are now his new king and allies. But honorable revenge must be served and fighting eventually breaks out when Hengest is remined of his obligation to his dead lord. The Danes finally kill Finn and take Hildeburh back with them to Denmark.

Once again this is a well-known story from Germanic leg-end. An alternate Old English version of the same story has happened to survive in the form of the poem titled *The Finns-burg Fragment* (or *The Fight at Finnsburg*).[14] This is a remnant of what likely was a longer poem (although probably not as long as *Beowulf*), and the treatment of the story in *Finnsburg* is much different: it is told from the Danish perspective and focuses on the crisis moment when, alone at night in the guest-hall in Frisia, the Frisians surprise-attack the Danes. Danish warriors step forward in succession and swear to do their duty to their lord and die bravely in hopeless defence. In feel and tone *Finnsburg* is much like *Maldon* or portions

---

14 Edited with full commentary in Klaeber, 273–90; translation in Heaney, NCE, 96–98. At only forty-five lines, the poem is missing beginning and ending.

of the *Waltharius*: a vivid poetic expression of the Germanic motif of "men dying at the side of their lord." Hildeburh is not mentioned in *Finnsburg* and therefore likely was not a main focus of its version of the story.

The *Beowulf*-poet easily could have chosen to present his version of the story in the same way as the *Fragment*: successive moments of heroic male bravery in the face of death. This would have seemed an appropriate choice for the *scop* as a celebration of Beowulf's victory. But no: strikingly, the poet chooses to tell the story through Hildeburh. In a familiar pattern, references to Hildeburh begin and end the episode. (In order to highlight that this is a poem-within-a-poem, Heaney shortens his lines and sets off the text with italics):

> *Hildeburh*
> > *had little cause*
> *to credit the Jutes:*
> > *son and brother,*
> *she lost them both*
> > *on the battlefield.*
> *She, bereft*
> > *and blameless, they*
> *foredoomed, cut down*
> > *and spear-gored. She,*
> *the woman in shock,*
> > *waylaid by grief,*
> *Hoc's daughter—*
> > *how could she not*
> *lament her fate*
> > *when morning came*
> *and the light broke*
> > *on her murdered dears?*
> > > (1070–78)

The episode begins by dwelling on Hildeburh's grief at the loss of her son and brother in the initial fighting. The next lines describe the truce and its terms and dilemmas; the oaths sworn on both sides. The midpoint of the episode pauses for the funeral cremation of the fallen:

> *A funeral pyre*
> > *was then prepared,*
> *effulgent gold*
> > *brought out from the hoard.*
> *The pride and prince*
> > *of the Shieldings lay*
> *awaiting the flame.* (1107–10)

Again the focus falls on Hildeburh, as the scene contains familiar elements in this tragic pattern: gold treasures, bloody bodies, fire, and a mourning woman caught up in events:[15]

> *Then Hildeburh*
> > *ordered her own*
> *son's body*
> > *be burnt with Hnaef's,*
> *the flesh on his bones*
> > *to sputter and blaze*
> *beside his uncle's.*
> > *The woman wailed*
> *and sang keens,*
> > *the warrior went up.* (1115–19)

The poet lingers on the bodies crumbling in the fire, a sign of tragedy in the poem:

> *... heads melted,*
> > *crusted gashes*
> *spattered and ran*
> > *bloody matter.* (1122–23)

The episode then details the long winter Hengest broods over his lot in Finn's home, until the dam breaks in the spring and the episode runs swiftly to its the end, with a focus on Hildeburh in its final lines:

---

15 On the mourning women image see Joyce Hill, "*Þæt wæs geomuru ides!* A Female Stereotype Examined," in *New Readings on Women in Old English Literature*, ed. Helen Damico and Alexandra Hennessey Olsen (Bloomington: Indiana University Press, 1990), 235–47.

> The wildness in them
> had to brim over.
> The hall ran red
> with blood of enemies.
> Finn was cut down,
> the queen brought away
> and everything
> the Shieldings could find
> inside Finn's walls—
> the Frisian king's
> gold collars and gem-
> stones—
> swept off to the ship.
> Over sea-lanes then
> back to Daneland
> the warrior troop
> bore that lady home. (1150–58)

The episode is structured around Hildeburh: she is given prominent place in the beginning, middle, and end; its tragic suffering is focused through her. Having lost her brother, husband, and son, she is carried back to her homeland, like the treasure looted from the Frisians. And like our other women, her final reactions are left opaque as she is swept along by events: we have no words or thoughts or final reactions from her, directly or indirectly expressed.

Grendel's Mother

Does even Grendel's mother fit into the same tragic pattern? Is she too a woman also caught up in the sweep of events, even as she tries to make the right choices? Very much so. The poem clearly depicts her as pulled into an analogous vendetta between Hrothgar and Grendel: in Grendel's "long and unrelenting feud" with Hrothgar, the monster "would never / parley or make peace with any Dane / nor stop his death-dealing nor pay the death-price" (153, 154–56). Grendel's mother's attack on Heorot is then motivated by revenge for her son's death:

> ... an avenger lurked and was still alive,
> grimly biding time. Grendel's mother,
> monstrous hell-bride, brooded on her wrongs.
> (1257–59)

We do get details here about her mind: she is suffering in her loss, brooding on her wrongs:

> But now his mother
> had sallied forth on a savage journey,
> grief-racked and ravenous, desperate for re-
> venge. (1276–78)

She is not as powerful a creature as her son; in her attack, she carries off one man and wants out quickly: "The hell-dam was in panic, desperate to get out, / in mortal terror the moment she was found" (1292–93). In the morning, Hrothgar tells Beowulf that "she has taken up the feud / because of last night, when you killed Grendel ... to avenge her kinsman's death" (1333–34, 1340). Even at the climactic moment of her fight with Beowulf, the poem draws attention to her motivation: "now she would avenge / her only child" (1546–47). Like the other women of the poem, Grendel's mother tries to navigate the violent retributions around her. All the essential images of this tragic pattern are there in her underwater home: a mutilated dead body (Grendel's); "treasure in abundance" (1612); fire—on the surface of the lake (1365–66) and in her hall ("firelight, / a gleam and a flare-up, a glimmer of brightness", 1516–17); and a woman caught up in unexpected tragic events.

Thus the poet has carefully engaged the women as a way to examine the tragic condition that can be the human predicament. Freawaru, Hygd, Wealhtheow, Hildeburh, and Grendel's mother: these women are at the epicentre of one of the poem's tragic patterns, as they try to play the cards they are dealt. As Eagleton notes: "A good deal of tragedy is about being trapped in irresolvable dilemmas, coerced into action by dully compulsive forces. Some tragic art affirms diversity, while some charts the dismal constraints of human existence, its dingy, monotonously repetitive dimensions, the alarming narrowness of our scope for free decision."[16] As I noted earlier, the poem's tragic tendencies do not only include the women: Beowulf and Hrothgar, for example are also epicentres of tragedy; the same can be said of Herebeald, eldest son of Hrothgar, killed accidentally by his younger brother Hæthcyn (2435-71); tragic events also overtake unnamed characters such as the Last Survivor and the unnamed father who sees his son die on the gallows (in the extended simile of lines 2446-62); moreover, the Geats and the Danes, collectively as groups, also arguably follow a tragic pattern. Tragic choices in the face of constraining events are not the sole province of the poem's women, but the poet carefully arranges these particular characters as part of a subtle tragic meditation.

At the end of the poem, an unnamed Geatish woman mourns for Beowulf at his funeral pyre, in much the same way that Hildeburh lamented her son and brother. We have a familiar scene one last time: the violated body, the treasures, the fire, and the mourning woman:

> A Geat woman too sang out in grief;
> with hair bound up, she unburdened herself
> of her worst fears, a wild litany
> of nightmare and lament: her nation invaded,
> enemies on the rampage, bodies in piles,
> slavery and abasement. Heaven swallowed the
> smoke. (3150-55)

This final anonymous woman almost seems to represent all the women who have come before in the poem. Like a Greek tragic chorus, these women stand in for the audience and comment on the action before us; in their plight—caught in the flux of events and trying to make their way through doubtful currents—they embody a humanist response to the poem's existential questions.

This is all pretty grim, I know; but the poem does offer hope as well. Poole notes that "The menace and promise of tragedy lie in this recognition of the sheer potentiality of all

---

16 Eagleton, *Sweet Violence*, 62.

the selves we might be, and of all the worlds we might make together or destroy together."[17] Tragedy is not all darkness; its darkness gains power by the way it reveals a better way, even if that way is foreclosed by the tragic conclusion. The darkness of tragedy is dependent upon some glimpse, however small, of consolation and light, or even the brief recognition of change. *Beowulf* shows us a dark vision, but in doing so it also declares that there is a world elsewhere.

---

[17] Poole, *Tragedy: Shakespeare and the Greek Example*, 2.

Chapter 4

Art and the Cunning of Form

So far, I have painted *Beowulf*'s humanist character in sombre tones: the poem's total vision of experience is riven by doubt; dwells upon the human dilemma of contingency; mourns the consequent tragedy of the human story. Our poem would still be a very great work of art if those characteristics were the limit of its vision. However, the relative pessimism of the poem is not its only experience: there is joy and delight here as well. This chapter will show that *Beowulf* ultimately, like many humanist endeavours, asserts the importance of Art as a counter to its darker imaginings.

One of the essential characteristics of humanism is its emphasis on human ingenuity; in the ability of human beings to use reason to make their way in the world and guide their endeavours; to rely upon innate human faculties as a guide to life and not to fall prey to that which is mystical, irrational, miraculous.[1] In more modern times this results in the humanist emphasis on empiricism, scientific method, and atheism. I submit that there is a *version* of this humanist impulse in *Beowulf*, most clearly in in the poem's love for what we might call the "cunning of form."[2] "Cunning" is generally a pejorative word now: it means using a skill in a secret or deceptive manner for the purposes of deceit. But "cunning" derives

---

1 See Davies, *Humanism*, 105–24; Law, *Humanism*, 1, 89–91.

2 The phrase was used by Kriss Basil in his 2002 Harvard PhD dissertation, "Narrative, Ethics, and the Cunning of Form."

from the Old English verb *cunnan*, "to know"; and "cunning" once denoted not deception, but rather knowledge, learning, wisdom, intelligence; a science (cf. Latin *scientia*), art, or a craft. "Cunning" was the knowledge of *how to do something*. So when I say *Beowulf* delights in the "cunning of form," I mean that the poem esteems the human shaping of the world through the creativity of the mind and skill of the hand. This is *Beowulf*'s version of the humanist allegiance to reason and rejection of the irrational.

The early medieval view of nature was not a Romantic one: nature was not the source of renewal and transcendence that it would be for Emerson and Thoreau; nature was a harsh force, held at bay by human ingenuity.[3] *Beowulf* finds joy and transcendence in the varied ways that human beings apply skill and creativity to shape the natural world around them and to live considered lives in the world. As Bruce Mitchell notes, *Beowulf*, in the end, is not exclusively bleak, because it "affirms that life is worth living. There is joy in ships and armour, in jewels and precious things, in warriors marching, in horse races and beer, in being a well-governed people."[4] The cunning of the poet, smith, shipwright, maker, artist, the cunning of the *faber*: all are aspects of the poem's humanism. There is surely delight in the cunning of form for its own sake; but, moreover, some voices of the poem tell us that the cunning of form can even extend life, bear the human presence beyond a single lifespan. Stories and poem outlive us; artistic objects are handed down, generation to generation, exceeding any one human life. The poem often marvels at this profound truth; for example, when the thief steals "the gold-plated cup" from the dragon-hoard, gives it to his lord, and

---

3 See generally Jennifer Neville, *Representations of the Natural World in Old English Poetry* (Cambridge: Cambridge University Press, 1999).

4 Bruce Mitchell, "'Until the Dragon Comes…'," 11. For illustrated introductions to the relevant material culture, see Leslie Webster, "Archaeology and *Beowulf*," in NCE, 199–230; and her *Anglo-Saxon Art* (Ithaca: Cornell University Press, 2012).

he and the poem pause to regard it: "His master gazed / on that find from the past for the first time" (2281–82, 2285–86).

This chapter will survey the poem's delight in all these forms of making, the poem's commitment to Art; and we will see that it is pervasive and a reason why the poem, for all its grim tones, has some sublime transcendence. But in *Beowulf* the darkness cannot be kept at bay for too long, even by the cunning of form. Humanism aligns itself with the innate capacities of human beings, but it also views those capacities with clear-eyed reason and attention to human failings; for Hamlet, the brave firmament above, fretted with golden fire, is to him only a foul and pestilent congregation of vapors; humanity is noble in reason and infinite in faculties, but is also nothing but dust. In the end, all of these examples of the cunning of form in *Beowulf* are also qualified in some way.

Poetry

Poetry itself—the skill of giving artistic order to verbal chaos—is an explicit subject of *Beowulf*.[5] *Beowulf* gives us several scenes of poetic composition and performance. It is clear that *Beowulf* draws extra attention to the very act of poetic composition itself as part of the formulaic theme of "joy in the hall." We are not even a hundred lines into the poem before the narrative gives us a scene of poetry-making. It is the sound of joyful poetic song in Heorot that angers Grendel; he hears a song of making, a poem of creation:

> ... the clear song of a skilled poet
> telling with mastery of man's beginnings,
> how the Almighty had made the earth
> a gleaming plain girdled with waters;

---

5 For a social and historical study of poets and poetry see Emily V. Thornbury, *Becoming a Poet in Anglo-Saxon England* (Cambridge: Cambridge University Press, 2014); for a study of the material/ manuscript facts of reading poetry see Daniel Donoghue, *How the Anglo-Saxons Read Their Poems* (Philadelphia: University of Pennsylvania Press, 2018).

> in His splendour He set the sun and the moon
> to be earth's lamplight, lanterns for men,
> and filled the broad lap of the world
> with branches and leaves; and quickened life
> in every other thing that moved. (90–98)

The court poet appropriately sings of world-creation at this very moment, when the narrative of the poem itself is still beginning. With its dim echoes of Genesis, the moment ties together the creation of our poem with creation of the world and the creation of the just-completed hall, Heorot.

After Beowulf's first encounter with Grendel, the poem gives us a remarkable scene in which the *scop* creates a new poem extemporaneously, praising Beowulf's deed, weaving it alongside the story of Sigemund from Germanic legend:

> Meanwhile, a thane
> of the king's household, a carrier of tales,
> a traditional singer deeply schooled
> in the lore of the past, linked a new theme
> to a strict metre. The man started
> to recite with skill, rehearsing Beowulf's
> triumphs and feats in well-fashioned lines,
> entwining his words. He told what he'd heard
> repeated in songs about Sigemund's exploits,
> all of those many feats and marvels .... (866–75)

The Old English word *scop* ("poet, singer") is related to the verb *scyppan*, meaning "to create, shape, make." This scene tells us that the *scop* creates by "linking a new theme / to a strict metre" (*word oþer fand / soðe gebunden*). Scholars argue over the exact meaning of these words, but the aesthetic intent driving them is clear, as is the notion that this is a new poem, about new events, to be added to the "lore of the past" and a complement to Beowulf's fame. Poetry and the telling of stories is a way to challenge death, for words and works to live on.

In the world of early medieval heroic culture, poetry is not just entertainment, but vital to bringing meaning to life: verbal art can be a secular, humanist source of transcendence.

Human lives extend beyond the grave through poetry: the poem's first lines tell us that "we" have all heard of the famous deeds of the Scyldings—through tales and poems. Some voices of *Beowulf* (but, importantly, not all) tell us that courageous deeds are the way to live on after death. For example, Hrothgar to Beowulf after he kills Grendel: "you have made yourself immortal / by your glorious action" (953–54); Beowulf's words to Hrothgar after Grendel's mother attacks:

> "For every one of us, living in this world
> means waiting for our end. Let whoever can
> win glory before death. When a warrior is gone,
> that will be his best and only bulwark." (1386–89)

The operative word in both of these passages is *dom*; *dom* is the honour, glory, and reputation that you achieve through noble and active striving in the world. However, what sustains and transmits *dom* across generations is the word: the words of story and song. That is why Beowulf's deeds are immediately transformed to poetry and placed alongside the legendary tales of Sigemund; his glory, his *dom*, now becomes part of that poetic tradition. Poetry in the poem is therefore humanist in that it is a way to defy death that does not proceed through supernatural means. Again, it is not the *only* voice in the poem speaking to such matters, and there are other perspectives presented that are diametrically opposed to this idea, but at these moments *Beowulf* asserts the humanist cunning of poetry.

The Hall

Old English poetry is shaped by ancient traditions of craftmanship; the *scop* finds the right words out of the pre-existing traditional store of words and binds them together truly (*soðe gebunden*), as a good craftsman works in wood or metal. In the beginning of the poem, the focus falls on the wondrous hall Heorot, a real-world counterpart to the universal world-creation sung of by the *scop*. Heorot was "meant to be a wonder of the world forever" (70), "the greatest house /

in the world" (145–46). In the great set piece as Beowulf and his men approach it for the first time, Heorot is simply one of the most beautiful wrought things depicted in the poem:

> They marched in step,
> hurrying on till the timbered hall
> rose before them, radiant with gold.
> Nobody on earth knew of another
> building like it. Majesty lodged there,
> its light shone over many lands. (306–11)

The hall is an important central symbol of community and joy in Old English poetry; shaped by human hands, the hall is a resplendent beauty compared to the action of the sun itself: "its light shone over many lands" (*lixte se leoma ofer landa fela*).[6]

Beowulf and Grendel damage Heorot, and the poem details the repairs as it is readied for renewed celebration and restored to its proper communal use:

> Then the order was given for all hands
> to help to refurbish Heorot immediately:
> men and women thronging the wine-hall,
> getting it ready. Gold thread shone
> in the wall-hangings, woven scenes
> that attracted and held the eye's attention.
> (990–95)

This passage could be explained as a matter of simple realism: they need to clean up before they can celebrate. However, it is also a moving figure for the cunning of form. Their hall, symbol of all their communal inspirations and aspirations, all that raises them up and makes them human, was corrupted, cursed, and haunted; it was then cleansed, but in doing so was damaged. As a human community, they all work together to restore it, pushing back again on the dark with the cunning of form, moving together to re-create its beauty, much as the

---

6 See Kathryn Hume, "The Concept of the Hall in Old English Poetry," *Anglo-Saxon England* 3 (1974): 63–74; T. A. Shippey, *Beowulf* (London: Arnold, 1978), 22–24.

woven threads of the wall hangings unite to create scenes that hold "the eye's attention." Busy creating art, they do not know that Grendel's mother awaits that night, but, for a moment, Heorot's light gleams out again across many lands.

Ships and Horses

Beowulf loves finely crafted ships and the skills of sea-voyaging. The poem begins with a mythic sea voyage: Scyld's arrival by sea as an infant and then his funeral back to "to the sea's flood" (30) in a ship loaded with treasure, a "gold standard up / high above his head" (47–48). Two other sea voyages punctuate the narrative: the journey of the Geats to Denmark (198–228), in which the ship's course is compared to a bird's flight: "Over the waves, with the wind behind her / and foam at her neck, she flew like a bird / until the curved prow had covered the distance (217–19); and then the return voyage (1888–1913):

> Right away the mast was rigged with its sea-shawl;
> sail-ropes were tightened, timbers drummed
> and stiff winds kept the wave-crosser
> skimming ahead; as she heaved forward,
> her foamy neck was fleet and buoyant,
> a lapped prow loping over currents,
> until finally the Geats caught sight of coastline
> and familiar cliffs. The keel reared up,
> wind lifted it home, it hit on the land. (1905–13)

The poem lovingly depicts the coursing voyages and the skilled tasks of readying the ship, moving it up onto the beach, disembarking. These scenes derive their energy from the essential interaction between human skill and the power of nature—the beautiful cunning ship not defying nature, but rather using and shaping it to human ends.

To these three voyages, we can perhaps add a fourth implied example at the end of the poem. Beowulf commands his people to bury him in a newly built barrow by the sea, to serve as a landmark for sailors:

> "Order my troop to construct a barrow
> on a headland on the coast, after my pyre has cooled.
> It will loom on the horizon at Hronesness
> and be a reminder among my people—
> so that in coming times crews under sail
> will call it Beowulf's Barrow, as they steer
> ships across the wide and shrouded waters." (2802–8)

Funerals of kings begin and end the poem. As an image, Scyld's death voyage combines the stasis of the grave with the movement of a ship; Beowulf's Barrow here has the same elements: it is a grave, a static construction, "as worthy of him as their workmanship could make it" (3162), but in its capacity as a sea-beacon to sailors it also gestures toward the movement and energy of a ship.

Horses function in a similar way in the poem; there is clear delight in the skill of horse-riding and of cunning gear, such as well-wrought saddles.[7] Placed in the aftermath of triumphs, scenes of horse-racing are a visual shorthand for celebration (863–66, 915–19, 1399–402). Horses and their gear are also splendid artisanal gifts:

> Next the king ordered eight horses
> with gold bridles to be brought through the yard
> into the hall. The harness of one
> included a saddle of sumptuous design ...
> (1034–37; see also 2163–66)

Like sailing, horse-riding is similarly a figure for the interaction between the forces of nature and human ingenuity; horses and bridles and saddles suggest, with fine economy, the relationship between nature and human craft: the wildness of the horse bridled for use by human skill.

---

7 On the horses in *Beowulf*, see Jennifer Neville, "Hrothgar's Horses: Feral or Thoroughbred?" *Anglo-Saxon England* 35 (2006): 131–57.

Treasure

No one can read *Beowulf* and not notice the poem is flush with treasure.[8] Treasure is diffused throughout the poem and there are also extended stately scenes of formal gift-giving and generous reward (e.g., 1019–52). I will note here just three representative types of treasured objects: the banner, the cup, and the necklace. Three banners, cunningly woven and public signs of victory, appear in *Beowulf*. A beautiful gold banner is set over Scyld's body on his funeral ship; Beowulf also receives "a gold standard as a victory-gift, / an embroidered banner" (1020–21) from Hrothgar; in the dragon's barrow, Wiglaf sees "a standard, entirely of gold, / hanging high over the hoard, / a masterpiece of filigree; it glowed with light ..." (2767–69). Ornamented cups are not just simple drinking vessels; cups are finely wrought ceremonial objects used in scenes of communal bonding (e.g., 614–30, 1160–93, 1980–83).[9] The poet lingers over the magnificent necklace given to Beowulf by Wealhtheow. The narrator calls it "the most resplendent / torque of gold I ever heard tell of / anywhere on earth or under heaven" (1194–96); he compares it to the mythic "necklace of the Brosings" (Old English *Brosinga men*; Old Norse *Brísinga men*, 1197–201). Beowulf then gives this necklace to Hygd (2172–74) and from her it moves to Hygelac, who dies with it on his breast (1202–14). We will see below that the joy in these objects is ultimately circumscribed, but it is clear that as each treasured object appears under the poet's eye, we are encouraged to marvel over the skill and ingenuity used to create objects of such beauty.

---

8 On the thematic significance of treasure in the poem, see Baker, *Honour, Exchange and Violence in* Beowulf, 35–76; for a broader perspective on the subject see Elizabeth M. Tyler, *Old English Poetics: The Aesthetics of the Familiar in Anglo-Saxon England* (York: York Medieval Press, 2006).

9 See Roberta Frank, "Three 'Cups' and a Funeral in *Beowulf*," in *Latin Learning and English Lore: Studies in Anglo-Saxon Literature for Michael Lapidge*, ed. Katherine O'Brien O'Keeffe and Andy Orchard, 2 vols. (Toronto: University of Toronto Press, 2005), 1:407–20.

War Gear

Swords and armour are utilitarian (their worth measured by their efficacy), but also beautiful products of the hand.[10] References to armour are many, but Beowulf's armour comes under special scrutiny: "his mighty, hand-forged, fine-webbed mail," fashioned by the legendary smith of Germanic myth, Weland (1443, 453); it preserves his life in the swimming match with Breca (550–54) and also saves him from Grendel's mother (1547–53), each time receiving extra lines of detailed description:

> "My armour helped me to hold out;
> my hard-ringed chain-mail, hand-forged and linked,
> a fine, close-fitting filigree of gold,
> kept me safe when some ocean creature
> pulled me to the bottom." (550–54)

When Beowulf puts on his gear to descend into Grendel's mere, his helmet also displays the cunning of form:

> It was of beaten gold,
> princely headgear hooped and hasped
> by a weapon-smith who had worked wonders
> in days gone by and adorned it with boar-shapes;
> since then it had resisted every sword. (1450–54)

Note the reference to the unnamed, long-dead maker of the helmet; the poem often invokes these vanished artisans, making clear that the cunning of form allows the human presence to outlive the short human life through poems, ships, swords, armour, helmets.

Swords are objects of artistic wonder, passed down the generations like any other treasure. There are many signif-

---

10 For a discussion of weapons and armour in the poem see Shippey's succinct analysis in *Beowulf*, 21–22 and Caroline Brady, "'Weapons' in *Beowulf*: An Analysis of the Nominal Compounds and the Poet's Use of Them," *Anglo-Saxon England* 8 (1979): 79–141. For general context see Hilda Davidson, *The Sword in Anglo-Saxon England: Its Archaeology and Literature* (Oxford: Clarendon Press, 1962).

icant swords in the poem: the sword placed on Hengest's lap to remind him of his duty; the Danish sword on the hip of a Heathobard that causes violence to break out in the Freawaru story; Wiglaf's sword (originally the sword of Eanmund) that kills the dragon; Hrethel's sword, "a gold-chased heirloom," "the best example / of a gem-studded sword in the Geat treasury" (2191–93) given to Beowulf by Hygelac; and Beowulf's own sword Naegling, a "keen-edged sword / an heirloom inherited by ancient right" (2562–63); and of course the giant-sword Beowulf finds in Grendel's home. We might pause over Hrunting, Unferth's sword, loaned to Beowulf when he attacks Grendel's mother. Hrunting is a "rare and ancient sword" (1458) and gets extra emphasis:

> The iron blade with its ill-boding patterns
> had been tempered in blood. It had never failed
> the hand of anyone who hefted it in battle,
> anyone who had fought and faced the worst
> in the gap of danger. This was not the first time
> it had been called to perform heroic feats.
>
> (1459–64)

The poet returns to Hrunting several times, as it fails and then is returned to Unferth (1520–33, 1659–60, 1807–12). Swords such as Hrunting rise almost to the level of characters in the poem: they have a complex being, an essential presence. Swords have a life of their own, as cunning objects that cross time, made by human hands and set free into the world to live and thrive and achieve glory (*dom*) or rust, break, and die.

The Cunning of Form and its Limits

And yet, for all the love of the faber's work, the cunning of form cannot completely escape the poem's melancholy. Yes, swords are glorious, each one "a smith's masterpiece" (673), but in *Beowulf* they are not usually represented as performing in superlative ways like Arthur's Excalibur or Roland's Durendal or Siegfried's Balmung; they are more often presented as failing. As we have seen, Hrunting has a long history of deadly beauty, but we only are allowed to see it fail in the poem, not succeed, against Grendel's mother:

> But he soon found
> his battle-torch extinguished: the shining blade
> refused to bite. It spared her and failed
> the man in his need. It had gone through many
> hand-to-hand fights, had hewed the armour
> and helmets of the doomed, but here at last
> the fabulous powers of that heirloom failed [*dom
> alæg*]. (1522–28)

Naegling as well, "infallible before that day," will not bite the dragon's head and then breaks (2575–86, 2677–82); even the giant sword melts away after its moment of triumph. How easy it would have been to show swords succeeding; how in keeping with heroic tradition it would have been to have a sword like Hrunting add to its *dom*, rather than fail. Indeed, the poem makes sure to tell us that this, unexpectedly, is the first time that Hrunting's *dom alæg*, its "glorious reputation failed."

Beowulf uses his ingenious, custom-made iron shield to protect him from the dragon's fire (2337–41), certainly a humanist application of reason to a problem of nature; but the poem includes this unusual plan, only to tell us that it did *not* work as its innovative fabers planned: "Yet his shield defended / the renowned leader's life and limb / for a shorter time than he meant it to" (2570–72). War-gear is beautiful, but is not always presented in a positive light; if not used honorably, it can be a mark of shame. When Wiglaf berates Beowulf's cowardly men, he focuses on their useless war-gear:

> "Anyone ready to admit the truth
> will surely realize that the lord of men
> who showered you with gifts and gave you the armour
> you are standing in—when he would distribute
> helmets and mail-shirts to men on the mead-benches,
> a prince treating his thanes in hall
> to the best he could find, far or near—
> was throwing weapons uselessly away." (2864–71)

Each of the arts we have examined receives some sort of qualification, some doubt, some lingering vestigial sense that there are limits to the cunning of form and its transcendence.

What about the necklace given by Wealhtheow to Beowulf, the one as glorious as the storied "necklace of the Brosings"? Beowulf gives it to Hygd, but then it is on Hygelac when he dies on his disastrous prideful raid against the Franks (1202–14). The necklace is thus beautiful, but its final image in the poem is on a dead king's body, a moment that also would begin a chain of terrible fortunes for the Geats. Yes, cups can be emblems of communal happiness, but remember that it is also specifically the theft of a cup (not some other object), "a gem-studded goblet," a "precious metalwork" (2217, 2230–31) from the hoard that brings about the dragon's wrath, Beowulf's death, and a bleak future for the Geats. All that misery, for a simple cup. Treasure can be a glorious vehicle for generosity, good when it flows and moves and circulates; but also a temptation to greed and pride and stasis, hoarding and death. A ship crosses the sea, flying like a bird across the whale-road, an emblem of life and movement and art; but we also remember Scyld's death ship carrying his body back to the dark. A hall like Heorot shines out in its glory across the land, but even as it rises, the poet can't resist casting a shadow, telling us it awaited "a barbarous burning" and that its "doom abided / but in time it would come" (81–85).

But what of poetry? True, the sound of the court poet, singing a song of creation, brings Grendel in from the wasteland, but that must be an exception. Surely the poem does not ever cast poetry in a negative light? But look closer and even poetic delight is qualified. Poetry bring joy, but not only joy; it can bring somber thoughts of grief and refresh painful memories. Beowulf tells Hygelac of the poetic celebrations in Heorot, but notes that such poetry also brought sadness to their hearts:

> "There was singing and excitement: an old reciter,
> a carrier of stories, recalled the early days.
> At times some hero made the timbered harp
> tremble with sweetness, or related true
> and tragic happenings; at times the king

> gave the proper turn to some fantastic tale,
> or a battle-scarred veteran, bowed with age,
> would begin to remember the martial deeds
> of his youth and prime and be overcome
> as the past welled up in his wintry heart."
>
> (2105–14; cf. 2444–62)

Poetry is the instrument to make heroic deeds live forever, certainly a positive value. But *Beowulf* tells us that poetry cuts both ways: the power of memory that it brings to bear captures all that is good and noble, but also raises sadder moments and more terrible emotions that perhaps would have been better lost. Liuzza makes this point when he details "the disruptive and violent potential of memory" in *Beowulf* and observes that "[t]he traces of the past in the present are not always happy ones, and memory's power can be centrifugal as well as centripetal, as likely to tear apart the hall as to preserve it."[11]

The Last Survivor

If there were one movement in the poem that would seem to capture all of these ambiguities about art and the cunning of form, it would be the history of the dragon's hoard. For three hundred years the dragon occupies an underground barrow. The dragon's lair seems to be a natural underground cave, an "earth-house" (2232) "on a wide headland / close to the waves" (2242–43). Other details seem to imply the barrow is the ruin of a skillful human construction: it has the "steep vaults of a stone-roofed barrow" (2212); the entrance is a "stone arch" (2545). As Beowulf lay dying, "He steadied his gaze / on those gigantic stones, saw how the earthwork / was braced with arches built over columns" (2717–19). The barrow is the *eald enta geweorc*, "the ancient work of giants,"

---

11 R. M. Liuzza, "*Beowulf*: Monuments, Memory, History," in *Readings in Medieval Texts: Interpreting Old and Middle English Literature*, ed. David Johnson and Elaine Treharne (Oxford: Oxford University Press, 2005), 91–108 at 97, 98.

a poetic formula used in other poems to describe cities or wondrous and imposing ruins from the past (Heaney translates as "immemorial howe," 2774). Thus the dragon's lair combines both the idea of the natural world and the skillful human shaping of that world.

Long ago, the poem tells us, the "Last Survivor" of a vanished people had buried their treasure here and lamented their extinction. The poem does not give either the people or the Last Survivor a name, keeping them anonymous, like the long-lost makers of other swords and helmets:

> ... long ago, with deliberate care,
> some forgotten person had deposited the whole
> rich inheritance of a highborn race
> in this ancient cache. Death had come
> and taken them all in times gone by
> and the only one left to tell their tale,
> the last of their line, could look forward to nothing
> but the same fate for himself ... (2233–40)

We then are pulled back in time, to the moment when the barrow has been completed by the Last Survivor, who then speaks final words, an inset poem of mourning; the lyric begins by addressing the personified earth itself, the barrow by the sea, ready for its treasure:

> "Now, earth, hold what earls once held
> and heroes can no more; it was mined from you first
> by honourable men. My own people
> have been ruined in war; one by one
> they went down to death, looked their last
> on sweet life in the hall." (2247–52)

A war has swept away his people, but all details are left abstract; sweet life in the hall, that image of communal making, is left desolate. The speaker then turns the focus on himself:

> "I am left with nobody
> to bear a sword or burnish plated goblets,
> put a sheen on the cup. The companies have departed."
>   (2252–54)

A parade of art objects begins: sword and cup, but no users. The human beings have departed that used those objects, draining part of their life away. The lyric then catalogues more treasures wasting away, each image encompassing the cunning of form in beauty and decay. As the items each in turn gleam before him in the present (which is the distant past, from the poem's narrative perspective), the speaker pictures their decay in the future (which is the immediate present, from the poem's narrative perspective):

> "The hard helmet, hasped with gold,
> will be stripped of its hoops; and the helmet-shiner
> who should polish the metal of the war-mask sleeps;
> the coat of mail that came through all fights,
> through shield-collapse and cut of sword,
> decays with the warrior. Nor may webbed mail
> range far and wide on the warlord's back
> beside his mustered troops. No trembling harp,
> no tuned timber, no tumbling hawk
> swerving through the hall, no swift horse
> pawing the courtyard. Pillage and slaughter
> have emptied the earth of entire peoples." (2255–66)

The lyric has already given us the empty hall and the unused cup and sword; now here in this catalog are all the other examples of the cunning of form, seen both in their glory and their desuetude: helmet and armour; horses pawing the courtyard; poetry and the harp ringing out in the hall. All caught in the moving dialect of presence and absence: they are present as material objects, but their decayed presence also conjures up the absence of human lives, like a ghostly echo.

His speech concluded, the Last Survivor takes to the paths of exile: "until death's flood / brimmed up in his heart" (2269–70). The decaying treasure returns near the end of the poem, when Wiglaf enters the barrow; in addition to the beautiful, glittering treasures, he sees also that it is

> packed with goblets and vessels from the past,
> tarnished and corroding. Rusty helmets
> all eaten away. Armbands everywhere,

> artfully wrought. How easily treasure
> buried in the ground, gold hidden
> however skilfully, can escape from any man! (2761–66)

With that final comment, the narrator is clearly, at the least, ambivalent about the treasure (it is also possible that the treasure has a curse upon it: 3051–75). As one of his last wishes, Beowulf wants to look upon the dragon's hoard; he tells Wiglaf that his death "will be easier / for having seen the treasure, a less troubled letting-go / of the life and lordship I have long maintained" (2749–51). When he sees the treasure, he gives thanks to God that he has won it for his people; the implication is that he believes it will benefit them in the future:

> "To the everlasting Lord of All,
> to the King of Glory, I give thanks
> that I behold this treasure here in front of me,
> that I have been allowed to leave my people
> so well endowed on the day I die." (2794–98)

Presumably Beowulf believes that even though he has died, there is some compensation, in that he has removed the threat of the dragon and at least won this magnificent fortune for his people. A lesser poem might show or at least imply that the treasure does benefit the Geats under their new leader, Wiglaf. But in some of the poem's last lines, at Beowulf's funeral, we learn that the Geats bury the gold with him, to rust uselessly in the earth once again, as the narrator's comment makes clear:

> And they buried torques in the barrow, and jewels
> and a trove of such things as trespassing men
> had once dared to drag from the hoard.
> They let the ground keep that ancestral treasure,
> gold under gravel, gone to earth,
> as useless to men now as it ever was. (3163–68)

There is something very moving in the way the poem strives to find faith in the human presence behind works of art, only to finally bury those same hopes beneath the ground in oblivion. It is a powerful, but melancholy, aesthetic.

Fred Robinson notes that in *Beowulf* "[t]he human essence is to be found in the artificial, and the works of men's hands not only express but actually help implement their desire for rational control."[12] Such desire for rational control defines, in part, the poem's humanist spirit, the way it tries to strive for something miraculous that is nevertheless human. But its other voices intervene, qualify, and circumscribe such strivings. In its embrace of Art and the cunning of form, *Beowulf* comes close to the tragicomic tones of something like Shakespeare's *The Winter's Tale*: where joy and happiness is rounded by sadness, where the magic of art partially redeems the world before the curtain can be drawn.

---

12 Robinson, Beowulf *and the Appositive Style*, 74.

Conclusion

By way of conclusion, let's look at one final scene of the poem, a moment that has always seemed central to me: Beowulf's retrieval of the giant-sword. It is the one moment in the story when a human ventures into the non-human world and comes back, bearing something rich and strange. The sword is "an ancient heirloom / from the days of the giants" (1558–59), larger than any mortal man could wield, except Beowulf. The sword enables him to kill Grendel's mother and behead Grendel. The sword-blade, however, melts away, and Beowulf carries back from the lair only Grendel's head and "the inlaid hilt / embossed with jewels" (1614–15). Beowulf brings both to Hrothgar and hands over the hilt, the "rare smithwork" (1679), to the king:

> Then the gold hilt was handed over
> to the old lord, a relic from long ago [*enta ærgeweorc*]
> for the venerable ruler. (1677–79)

Hrothgar looks at the hilt, "that relic of old times" (*ealde lafe*), and the hilt delivers a message:

> It was engraved all over
> and showed how war first came into the world
> and the flood destroyed the tribe of giants.
> They suffered a terrible severance from the Lord;
> the Almighty made the waters rise,
> drowned them in the deluge for retribution.
> In pure gold inlay on the sword-guards

> there were rune-markings correctly incised,
> stating and recording for whom the sword
> had been first made and ornamented
> with its scrollworked hilt. (1688–98)

We do not quite know if "engraved" (OE *writen*) means the hilt has writing on it or a pictorial representation of God's destruction of the giants in the Genesis Flood (probably the latter). Runes on the hilt mark out the name of the sword's maker or owner. We also do not know if Hrothgar (or any other character) can "read" the hilt, if writing is indeed on it. But the hilt itself seems to provoke Hrothgar's long central speech (1698–1784), in which he muses upon many things including pride, death and mutability: the "hard reversal (*edwenden*) / from bliss to grief" (1774–75). He marvels how God grants happiness to a man for so long that he cannot imagine any end to it, cannot think of life ever being any other way (1724–39). But then change inevitably comes upon us all.

This scene touches on all our themes. There is doubt: Who made the sword or for whom? Does Hrothgar understand the story on the hilt? What is the "message" of the hilt and how does it relate to Hrothgar's speech? There is contingency: No one expected the existence of a weapon like this, much less its presence at Beowulf's hour of dire need. No one expects its blade to melt away. Engraved on the hilt is a primal legend of unexpected and unprecedented disaster: the Great Flood. There is tragedy: the hilt, passed between Beowulf and Hrothgar, marks the transition point from the suffering and deaths of the Danes in the first half of the poem to the sufferings of the Geats to come in the second half; the partial remnant of a sword standing for the ruined lives caught up in tragedy's causality. There is, of course, also Art and the cunning of form: the hilt is a beautiful and wondrous object, made by a long-vanished smith; but it is also now a partial and ruined object of cunning.

Beowulf is a superb work of humanist thought; it is a poem of complex and contradictory voices and perspectives. Indeed, its energy as a humanist work derives from its imperfect tension between secular and transcendent sources of human meaning. It achieved this complexity probably through a mix of artistic ambition and skill, impersonal and traditional cultural forces, and even just happenstance. If the reader is open-minded, humble, and accepting; willing to take a chance to be changed and transformed in the reading moment; able to recognize glimpses of a different self and see existential questions in the reading moment; then such a reader can find a deep and moving encounter with the humanist *Beowulf*. We all wrestle with doubt; we all make our way in a world of random events that threaten, at times, to overwhelm us and those we love in tragedy; and we all strive through the skill of hand, mind, and thought—sometimes bravely, sometimes fearfully—for some stay against the outer dark, even if we cannot see all ends.

Further Reading

I noted in the Introduction that anyone I have cited throughout this book has written more on *Beowulf*; I encourage you to seek out their work. I have therefore kept this list brief, generally concentrating on accessible works that enhance the literary appreciation of the poem.

Translations and Editions (in addition to the Heaney translation)

Fulk, R. D., Robert E. Bjork, and John D. Niles, eds. *Klaeber's Beowulf*, 4th ed. Toronto: University of Toronto Press, 2008.
    The authoritative scholarly edition, with a wealth of material for further study in its densely packed pages.

Garmonsway, G. N. and Jacqueline Simpson, trans. *Beowulf and its Analogues*. London: Dutton, 1968.
    Excellent prose translation of *Beowulf*, along with other relevant Germanic sources in translation.

Liuzza, R. M., ed. and trans. *Beowulf*, 2nd ed. Peterborough: Broadview, 2013.
    Accurate and poetic translation with excellent introduction and supporting materials; Old English text on the facing-pages.

Williamson, Craig, trans. *The Complete Old English Poems* (Philadelphia: University of Pennsylvania Press, 2017).
> Excellent poetic translations of the entire poetic corpus, including *Beowulf*.

Scholarly Handbooks

Bjork, Robert E. and John D. Niles, eds. *A* Beowulf *Handbook*. Lincoln: University of Nebraska Press, 1997.
> Well-organized survey essays by many hands on standard scholarly subjects.

Orchard, Andy. *A Critical Companion to* Beowulf. Cambridge: Brewer, 2003.
> A comprehensive scholarly study guide, with thorough bibliographic notes and indexes.

Essay Collections

Baker, Peter S., ed. *The* Beowulf *Reader*. New York: Garland, 2000.
> Essential and well-chosen articles, designed to represent a variety of approaches and subjects.

Chickering, Howell, Allen J. Frantzen and R. F. Yeager, eds. *Teaching Beowulf in the Twenty-First Century*. Tempe: Arizona Center for Medieval and Renaissance Studies, 2014.
> A variety of useful essays on materials and approaches to teaching the poem.

Fulk, R. D., ed. *Interpretations of* Beowulf*: A Critical Anthology*. Bloomington: Indiana University Press, 1991.
> An excellent collection, similar to Baker (above), but nicely complementary.

Joy, Eileen A. and Mary K. Ramsey, eds. *The Postmodern Beowulf: A Critical Casebook*. Morgantown: West Virginia University Press, 2006.
>
> A well-planned collection dedicated to literary/critical approaches to the poem such as psychoanalysis, gender studies, and eco-criticism.

Remein, Daniel C. and Erica Weaver, eds. *Dating Beowulf: Studies in Intimacy*. Manchester: Manchester University Press, 2020.
>
> A good recent collection of analyses of the poem from a variety of current literary/critical perspectives.

Monographs

Brodeur, Arthur. *The Art of Beowulf*. Berkeley: University of California Press, 1959.
>
> Elegant exposition of the poem's style and themes.

Damico, Helen. *Beowulf's Wealhtheow and the Valkyrie Tradition*. Madison: University of Wisconsin Press, 1984.
>
> Pioneering book on the women of the poem and underrated as far as its ability to place the poem in its Germanic contexts.

Deskis, Susan. *Beowulf and the Medieval Proverb Tradition*. Tempe: Arizona Center for Medieval and Renaissance Studies, 1996.
>
> Learned intertextual study of the poem's relationship to the wisdom literature tradition.

Forni, Kathleen. *Beowulf's Popular Afterlife in Literature, Comic Books, and Film*. New York: Routledge, 2018.
>
> A comprehensive introduction to and analysis of *Beowulf* adaptations.

Greenfield, Stanley. *Hero and Exile: The Art of Old English Poetry*, ed. George H. Brown (London: Hambledon, 1989).
>
> Collects the *Beowulf* essays (and others) by one of the most elegant and humane critics of the poem.

Irving, Edward B., Jr. *A Reading of* Beowulf. New Haven: Yale University Press, 1968.

  Classic and elegant literary analysis of the poem.

Niles, John D. Beowulf: *The Poem and Its Tradition*. Cambridge, MA: Harvard University Press, 1983.

  Important and comprehensive study of the poem, particularly good on the oral-formulaic background.

Overing, Gillian. *Language, Sign, and Gender in* Beowulf. Carbondale: Southern Illinois University Press, 1990.

  The first monograph to deliver a post-structuralist feminist reading of the poem.

Owen-Crocker, Gale H. *The Four Funerals in* Beowulf: *And the Structure of the Poem*. Manchester: Manchester University Press, 2000.

  Excellent interdisciplinary study incorporating insights from archaeology and material culture.

Robinson, Fred C. Beowulf *and the Appositive Style*. Knoxville: University of Tennessee Press, 1985.

  Influential compact study of the poem's style that branches out to a broader argument about the poem's meaning.

Shippey, T. A. *Beowulf*. London: Arnold, 1978.

  Wonderful extremely short study with insights on every page. Free for download off Shippey's academia.edu webpage.

Articles

Bennett, Helen. "The Female Mourner at Beowulf's Funeral: Filling in the Blanks/Hearing the Spaces." *Exemplaria* 4 (1992): 35–50.

  Influential feminist analysis.

Bjork, Robert E. "Speech as Gift in Beowulf." *Speculum* 69 (1994): 993–1022.
> Detailed study of speeches and eloquence in the poem.

Chance, Jane. "The Structural Unity of *Beowulf*: The Problem of Grendel's Mother." *Texas Studies in Language and Literature* 22 (1980): 287–303; repr in NCE, 153–168.
> Influential analysis of Grendel's mother from a feminist perspective.

Dockray-Miller, Mary. "Beowulf's Tears of Fatherhood." *Exemplaria* 10, no. 1 (1998): 1–28; repr. in *The Postmodern* Beowulf, ed. Joy and Ramsey, 439–466.
> Nuanced psychoanalytic and gender-based analysis of Hrothgar.

Earl, James. "The Forbidden *Beowulf*: Haunted by Incest," *PMLA* 125, no. 2 (2010): 289–305.
> One of two essays (see below) by Earl that place the poem in the context of its Germanic analogues with great critical intelligence.

——. "The Swedish Wars in Beowulf." *JEGP* 114, no. 1 (2015): 32–60.

Frank, Roberta. "The *Beowulf* Poet's Sense of History" in *The Wisdom of Poetry: Essays in Early English Literature in Honor of Morton W. Bloomfield.* Edited by Lawrence D. Benson and Siegfried Wenzel, 53–65. Kalamazoo: Medieval institute, 1982). Repr. in NCE, 168–82.
> Learned and graceful essay by one of the very best literary critics of Old English poetry.

Georgianna, Linda. "King Hrethel's Sorrow and the Limits of Heroic Action in *Beowulf*." *Speculum* 62 (1987): 829–50.
> Nuanced critical study of heroism and its ambiguities.

Harris, Joseph. *"Beowulf* in Literary History" *Pacific Coast Philology* 17 (1982): 16–23; repr. in *Interpretations of* Beowulf, ed. Fulk, 235–41.
> Compact and convincing intertextual study of the poem as a blend of many Germanic literary genres.

Lerer, Seth. "'*On Fagne Flor*': The Postcolonial *Beowulf*: from Heorot to Heaney" in *Postcolonial Approaches to the European Middle Ages: Translating Cultures.* Edited by Ananya Jahanara Kabir and Deanne Williams, 77–102. Cambridge: Cambridge University Press, 2005.
> Survey and analysis *Beowulf* as a postcolonial text.

Osborn, Marijane. "The Great Feud: Scriptural History and Strife in *Beowulf*" (1978), repr. in Baker, ed. *Basic Readings*, 111–25 and NCE, 139–53.
> Literary reading that also incorporates the poet's attitude toward Christianity, much like Robinson.

Price, Basil Arnould. "Potentiality and Possibility: An Overview of *Beowulf* and Queer Theory." *Neophilologus* 104, no. 3 (2020): 391–400.
> A recent thorough and insightful history of queer theory approaches to the poem.

Saltzman, Benjamin A. "Secrecy and the Hermeneutic Potential in *Beowulf*." *PMLA* 133, no. 1 (2018): 36–55.
> Eloquent analysis of the role secrecy plays in the poem and in its critical responses.

Tolkien, J. R. R. "*Beowulf*: The Monsters and the Critics." *Proceedings of the British Academy* 22 (1936): 245–95; repr. in Fulk, *Interpretations*, 14–44 and in NCE, 111–38.
> Long and chatty at times, but still absolutely essential reading with important points well-expressed.